D1614947

EDINBURGH UNIVERSITY LIBRARY
30150 002777321

Henry Vaughan

Poet of Revelation

by

Noel Kennedy Thomas

Dr Noel K. Thomas was for twenty-six years (until 1985) Head of the Department of English at Westhill College, affiliated to the University of Birmingham. His special research interests have included seventeenth century literature, Shakespeare, twentieth century drama and religious poetry of all periods. Dr. Thomas has been a frequent lecturer abroad, in Scandinavia, the United States, South America and Southern Africa. In 1985 he published a book of travel, *The Enchanted Land, A Journey Through Northern Cyprus.*

Henry Vaughan

Poet of Revelation

Silex Scintillans:
or
SACRED POEMS
and
Private Ejaculations
By
Henry Vaughan Silurist
LONDON Printed by T.W. for H. Blunden at ye Castle in Cornehill. 1650

Noel Kennedy Thomas

CHURCHMAN PUBLISHING
1986

Henry Vaughan
Poet of Revelation
was first published in 1986 by
Churchman Publishing Limited
117 Broomfield Avenue
Worthing
West Sussex
BN14 7SF

and distributed to the book trade by

Bailey Bros. & Swinfen Limited
Warner House
Folkestone
Kent
CT19 6PH

Churchman Publishing are represented in
Paris, Wellington N.Z., and Winnipeg

ISBN 1 85093 042 2

Filmset by Northumberland Press Limited,
Gateshead, Tyne and Wear
Printed in Great Britain by Paradigm Print,
Gateshead, Tyne and Wear

To the memory of my father
who had some comprehension
of 'the world of light'.

CONTENTS

PREFACE

In 1978 the Brecknock Society invited me to speak at the formal commemoration of the death of Henry Vaughan. I accepted the invitation and on April 23rd of that year, in Llansantffraed Church, very close to the poet's birth-place at Scethrog, I gave the address on 'Aspects of Revelation in Vaughan's Poetry'. In the years which followed, I widened and deepened my approach into a full re-appraisal of Vaughan's religious work, but the note of revelation, which seemed to me to be missing from Vaughan criticism, remained absolutely central. It is pleasant to record, therefore, that the Brecknock Society, which has done a good deal to develop interest in Vaughan, especially in Wales, and to honour one of their most famous native sons, provided, in one sense, the initial impetus for my work.

Inevitably, my other debts are many and it is impossible to acknowledge them all here. But I am especially grateful to my friend, Olwen Davies of Trefecca, so near to the heart of the Vaughan country, for all the help and encouragement she has given me. Another close friend, Margaret Robbins of Bath, very kindly typed out much of the original material; I am indebted to her for all her patience and hard work. Audrey Allen and Robin Schafer have given considerable assistance with the arrangements for the final manuscript, and for this I am most grateful. Among the many colleagues in Birmingham with whom I have discussed Vaughan's work, I must mention especially Robert Wilcher. His insight into various aspects of seventeenth century literature has been stimulating and his views on Vaughan clear and relevant.

Most valuable of all, David Merchant, a close colleague and friend for many years, has made many perceptive comments during the writing of this book and has assisted greatly with the reading of the final proofs.

Finally, I must record that much of this book was written on a remote and very beautiful farm in the mountains of Southern Swaziland. To my hosts and good friends, Springh and Eily Murphy, my thanks for their hospitality and kindness.

N.K.T
Birmingham, 1986

INTRODUCTION

Henry Vaughan has not on the whole been well treated by literary critics. The most usual interpretation of his poetry, both in general literary histories of the seventeenth century and specific critiques of his poetry, is that it is the work of a man who had brilliant mystic flashes, but these were not usually sustained or properly developed. Thus Helen C. White finds that 'his sensitivity outreaches his power of analysis, and his best intuitions would seem to come in a flash and all too often to vanish again when he tries to hold them or to fit their vague implications to a preconceived scheme.'[1]

Miss White is at least aware that Vaughan was deeply conscious of the social and political problems as he wrote, although she implies that such considerations do not enter into his finest work. Other critics of Vaughan seem almost completely unaware of the tensions of the Civil War and the Commonwealth period and their influence on the shaping of Vaughan's poetry. R.A. Durr, for example, sees Vaughan almost entirely as a mystic, and isolates his poetry almost entirely from the period in which it was written. He gives a long critique of one of Vaughan's finest lyrics, 'The Proffer', and makes only one single brief reference to 'the Commonwealth'. [2]His entire treatment of the poet re-enforces the impression that Vaughan's creative life was somehow divorced from the world, and that his inspiration was at its best when he sought refuge from the world.

E.C. Pettet, while giving considerable insight into the patterns of Vaughan's religious experience, also lays emphasis upon the quality of his mysticism. Nor does he pay any close attention to the social, political or ecclesiastical influences upon him. He notes very briefly that in the second 'Day of

[1] *The Metaphysical Poets*, A Study in Religious Experience, Macmillan, New York, (1956), p. 284.

[2] *On the Mystical Poetry of Henry Vaughan*, Harvard, Massachusetts, (1962), p. 108.

Judgement' poem in *Silex Scintillans*, Part Two, Vaughan 'thinks of punishment falling on the Puritans for their "forgeries" and "impious wit" rather than on sinners like himself', but there is no appreciation of the scale and scope of Vaughan's political interest. [1]

A much earlier critic, Edmund Blunden, is much more aware of the significance of political references in Vaughan's work. He gives clear and relevant illustrations from 'The Constellation' and 'The Proffer' to support his argument that the age had induced in Vaughan a 'passionate distress of mind'. [2] But his treatment, though sound and very relevant, is brief and sketchy.

Vaughan's principal biographer, F.E. Hutchinson, gives an adequate treatment of the Puritan period but keeps it well away from his main consideration of *Silex Scintillans.* He does acknowledge some of the political influences on Vaughan but regrets 'that the calm and remote air of his divine poems and devotional pieces should so often be ruffled by these political and ecclesiastical outbursts.' [3]

Rudrum has plainly seen the link between the eschatological aspects of Vaughan's work and the Civil War but has given no substantial treatment of it. [4]

In my exploration of Vaughan's religious verse I shall argue strongly that it is not only most unwise to separate the social and political issues of his age from his poetry, but that they constitute one of the greatest single influences upon him, to such an extent that it is simply not possible to appreciate his real worth as a religious poet unless one starts by examining in detail the effect of the Civil War and the Commonwealth period on his mind and art, and especially the impact which these events had upon Vaughan's own county of Breconshire.

The terrible tumult and bitterness of the sixteen forties and early fifties are not merely the background of *Silex Scintillans*; they provide so many of the tensions and conflicts of much of his major work, and influence his imagery and thought very deeply throughout the whole book. It is astonishing that

[1] *Of Paradise and Light*, Cambridge, (1960), p. 205.
[2] *On the Poems of Henry Vaughan*, London, (1927), p. 33.
[3] *Henry Vaughan, A Life and Interpretation*, Oxford, (1947), p. 109.
[4] A. Rudrum, *Writers of Wales, Henry Vaughan*, University of Wales Press, (1981).

critics and scolars have ignored this quite central aspect of Henry Vaughan. In the work of Puritan poets of the period, scholars have been extremely quick to note the political inferences and implications. But Vaughan the Royalist and champion of the cause of Anglicanism, has until very recently been pushed aside and forgotten.

The second main failure of Vaughan criticism is the unwillingness, or perhaps unpreparedness of scholars to appreciate just how wide and deep the influence of the authorized version of the Bible is upon Vaughan. It may well be that the much slighter influences of Platonism, Hermeticism and nature mysticism have distracted critics for so long. But in fact the contribution of the Bible to *Silex Scintillans* is absolutely massive. There is direct Biblical imagery and thought in an overwhelming number of the lyrics which make up the collection. And Vaughan's use of the Bible is more subtle and complex than even George Herbert's. George Herbert rarely draws from so many different parts of the Bible in his treatment of a single poem as does Vaughan. It is not uncommon for Henry Vaughan to use at least six different books of the Bible in the space of twenty or thirty lines. His lyric 'Religion' draws directly on *Genesis, Numbers, Kings,* the *Book of Psalms,* and the gospels of both *Mark* and *John* in the New Testament, quite apart from indirect references and suggestions from several other Biblical sources.

Indeed if any one single fact emerges from a close study of the Biblical thought and imagery of *Silex Scintillans* it is that Vaughan uses the Bible in all its colour and vitality to such tremendous effect that it is very difficult to think of any other religious poet writing in English who surpasses him. And although a number of critics have acknowledged some Biblical influence there has been no recognition of its enormous scope or scale, and very little appreciation of the way he re-lives some of the major experiences of the Old Testament and the New in terms of his own troubled experience in seventeenth century Puritan Britain.

A good deal of my exploration into the nature of Vaughan's religious experience is therefore necessarily devoted to the obvious links between Vaughan's perception of social and political events and his direct reading and use of the Scriptures. All through *Silex Scintillans* there is a poignant cry for deliverance, not only from the individual sin, which any Christian must utter, but from the bonds of a wider oppression and a deeper captivity. And his use of the apocalyptic sections of the Bible, and especially the *Book of Revelation*, is most marked. This is no accident. Vaughan sees in the desperation and excitement of John's vision from Patmos something of his own need for release from the sadness and oppression of spirit which he experiences so clearly.

If these essential aspects of Henry Vaughan's poetry had been grasped and explored more fully, his uniqueness as a religious poet would have become much more clear. Literary historians would have stopped treating him as in large part a copy of Herbert, and even his admirers would have to re-examine their view of him as a solitary nature mystic who sought to escape from the world around him.

Strangely the particular link with George Herbert which has received least attention is possibly the most important of all, and that is the common bond of Anglicanism. Vaughan's proclamation of the traditional, and for him eternal, truths of the Anglican ritual was undoubtedly a means of keeping alive his own faith not only in the true Church but in the King as Head of it, and thus building through his poetry a living memorial to the monarch who had died such a cruel death just as the poet was beginning *Silex Scintillans*. Undoubtedly Herbert's piety and his quietism attracted him strongly, but it was Herbert's continual celebration of the ordinary, everyday Anglican ritual and practice which served Vaughan with the political material he needed in facing a Puritan regime which, especially in Breconshire, had so savagely swept away the old Anglican order, and the stability and serenity which they had symbolized in the community.

But in most other respects, despite his many borrowings from Herbert, Henry Vaughan is utterly different from the man he so much admired, and his reputation as a poet has, on the whole, been damaged by the constant comparison with Herbert. In the first place he has far less interest in narrative than Herbert, and when he does attempt it, his lyrics often tend to become too complex and sometimes even tortuous. But he has much more obvious dramatic power than Herbert, and his capacity to dramatize the spiritual phases of his own life in the most vivid Biblical language and emotion places him immediately in a different area than the earlier poet.

Secondly he has a sharp and persistent awareness of political and social issues which is utterly different than Herbert. Although Herbert was certainly aware of alien creeds and attitudes developing within the Church and Society he faces none of the acute moral and spiritual dilemmas which confronted Vaughan. So that the direct employment of the Bible, and especially the prophetic and apocalyptic parts of it as a weapon of attack against his enemies, belongs to Vaughan, as it never did to Herbert, and it completely changes the nature and tone of his devotional verse.

But thirdly and finally I believe that Vaughan is not in any full sense a metaphysical poet, and it is misleading, to say the least, to include him in the general category of metaphysical poets, simply because he used, as did Donne, Herbert and others, some metaphysical conceits. First and foremost Henry Vaughan is a poet of revelation who speaks of the judgement of God at a time when he believed that nothing other than that prophetic judgement could rescue the soul of his people from falsehood, hypocrisy and violence in the social and political fabric of the nation.

It is the consistency and thoroughness of his revelation which mark his distinctiveness and value as a religious poet. Far from being a poet who can give us only brilliant flashes which are never integrated, I believe that Vaughan uses the Bible, Nature, and his own life to illustrate in great fullness his vision of Eternity.

This re-appraisal of his religious poetry is, therefore, most of all a plea for Vaughan to be examined on his own terms, not as a member of a group of metaphysical poets, or as an isolated mystic (which he certainly was not) but as a man who used all the sharpness and majesty of Biblical prophecy and apocalypse to bring his bitter and divided nation back to sanity, truth and righteousness under God. And in the realization of this vision I believe his poetic achievement is very great indeed, much more substantial than is normally claimed for him. So clear was his insight, and passionate his message that he must rank as one of the two or three finest religious poets in the history of our literature.

NOTE. All references to Vaughan's poetry and prose, are taken from L. C. Martin, *The Works of Henry Vaughan*, Oxford University Press, 1957.

POEMS DISCUSSED IN THE TEXT

(Those poems marked with an asterisk are the ones most often included in anthologies)

From 'Silex Scintillans', Part Two:

I

'OUR SAD CAPTIVITY'

Henry Vaughan grew up to manhood in the Breconshire of the sixteen thirties, the years of the gathering storm. Religious and political dissent were growing rapidly and the seeds of Parliament's quarrel with the king were sown in the developing conflicts of these years. And throughout this period the steady growth of Puritan ideas and congregations was sharpening the issues which would divide the country only a few years later.

Vaughan's years in London, probably from 1640 to 1642, must have left an abiding impression upon his mind. On October 22nd, 1640, an excited crowd broke into the Court of High Commission, and made its work impossible. The following month the Long Parliament impeached Strafford, and he was later committed to the Tower. In April of 1641, the Parliament passed the Bill of Attainder against Strafford, and on May 10th, after scenes of great agitation and violence, the King was forced to agree to Strafford's execution.

It would have been absolutely impossible for Vaughan to have been unaware of the seriousness of what was happening, and very difficult indeed for him not to have taken sides. Coming, as he did, from a strong Anglican and Royalist tradition, he must have been appalled by what he saw, and there seems no reason to doubt Hutchinson's view that Vaughan's 'detestation of "the populacy", which is constantly found in his secular and even in his religious verse, dated from these events of 1641.'[1]

It is significant that the longest poem in his first collection, *Poems, with the Tenth Satyre of Iuvenal Englished*, has an unmistakeable attack upon the Parliamentarians for their behaviour, and especially for the murder of Strafford. 'A Rhapsodie', written after a meeting with friends in the Globe Taverne, uses Roman history to veil, albeit very thinly, his sense of outrage. Vaughan proposes three toasts. The first

[1] Hutchinson, op. cit., p. 42.

celebrates Caligula's affront to the Senate of Rome by making his horse a Senator. Vaughan uses the Roman Senate to express his anger at the actions of Parliament. In the second toast Vaughan again indicts the Parliament and uses the figure of Caesar to symbolize King Charles I's attempts to arrest five members of Parliament in January, 1641:

> Now crown the second bowle, rich as his worth,
> I'le drinke it to; he! that like fire broke forth
> Into the Senates face, crost Rubicon,
> And the States pillars, with their Lawes thereon:
> And made the dull gray beards, & furr'd gowns fly
> Into *Brundusium* to consult, and lye:
>
> (p. 11, ll.51–56)

The analogy is not historically very accurate, but that is far less important than the fact that Vaughan feels so passionately about the behaviour of the Parliamentarians that he enters into the details of the long and bitter conflict as it was unfolding in 1641. In the final toast, to 'brave *Sylla*', Vaughan clearly commemorates the death of Strafford. Once again the historical parallel is a very rough one, but it at least makes the point that Sulla, like Strafford, was the upholder of the Patrician class, and thus a target for the rage of the people:

> This to brave *Sylla*! why should it be sed,
> We drinke more to the living, then the ded?
> Flatt'rers, and fooles doe use it: Let us laugh
> At our owne honest mirth; for they that quaffe
> To honour others, doe like those that sent
> Their gold and plate to strangers to be spent:
>
> (p. 11, ll.57–62)

If Vaughan showed this degree of involvement in public affairs, and personal passion in the Royalist cause, so early in his career, it is inconceivable that the anguished years which followed, and especially his own part in the Civil War, did not affect him very deeply. Indeed, two of the finest poems in 'Olor Iscanus' reveal great compassion for those who have been killed in the battles of the Civil War. 'An Elegie on the death of Mr. R. W. ...' is a most moving lament not only for the man but for the terrible times through which he had lived. And his tribute is touched not only by a deeply felt personal emotion but by a bitter attack on the hypocrisy of the Puritans who have, in Vaughan's view, confused the good of the people with their own selfish aims:

> He knew no *fear* but of his *God*; yet durst
> No injurie, nor (as some have) e'r purs't
> The sweat and tears of others, yet would be
> More forward in a royall gallantrie
> Than all those vast pretenders, which of late
> Swell'd in the ruines of their King and State.
> He weav'd not *Self-ends*, and the *Publick* good
> Into one piece, nor with the peoples bloud
> Fill'd his own veins;
>
> (p. 50, ll.41–49)

Clearly this is not the poetry of a man unaffected by the sorrows of his age. On the contrary, it shows strong and direct emotional involvement. The second, 'An Elegie on the death of Mr. R. Hall, slain at Pontefract, 1648', shows the same personal sincerity and passionate involvement in the tragedy of the period. In addition it underlines Vaughan's distress at the damage being done to the true Church of England. R. Hall was very probably a clergyman and Vaughan feels justified in referring to his death as '*Martyrdome*' (p. 58, 1.18). There is, moreover, a considerable political sharpness to this lament, and Vaughan's ending reminds us, not for the last time in his poetry, that it is those who have died in the cause of King and true Church who are the 'Saints' and not the self-styled 'Saints' of Cromwell's militia:

> Since then (thus flown) thou art so much refin'd,
> That we can only reach thee with the mind,
> will not in this *dark* and *narrow glasse*,
> Let thy scant *shadow* for *Perfections* passe,
> But leave thee to be read more high, more queint,
> In thy own bloud a *Souldier* and a *Saint*.
>
> (p. 59, ll.69–74)

When one turns to Vaughan's major work, *Silex Scintillans*, it becomes apparent that far from avoiding the tragic events of the Civil War, some of his finest poetry was written as a direct response to the difficulties and problems which a new political regime had thrust upon him, his family and his friends. Indeed, his own inner religious conflicts must be seen in the immediate context of a wider struggle against the Puritan Commissioners and their agents, of whom he did not approve and whose work he plainly considered to be a work of darkness, not of light. They were 'Commission'd by a black self-wil' (p. 470, l.37). It is therefore a double captivity of which he speaks in *Silex Scintillans*. There are at least nine poems in the first part, and thirteen in the second part, in which political material is used quite substantially and openly in the argument. But there are many others where the occasional mention or inference betrays Vaughan's constant concern with the situation as it existed not only in the country as a whole but especially in his own native Breconshire.

It is therefore essential to examine in some detail what was happening in Vaughan's own county in the years immediately following the collapse of the King's military hopes in Midsummer, 1646, and especially the ferment in the Church, and the Second Civil War in 1648. Some of the poems from the first part of *Silex Scintillans*, which he was writing during 1648 and 1649, must be looked at in that context. Before he wrote the poems which are included in the second part of the work the new Puritan regime had introduced the Act of Propagation of 1650. So controversial was this piece of legislation that it caused a furore of protest throughout the Principality and it was particularly disliked and contested in Breconshire. It is very important to take detailed note of the act and its main consequences before examining some of the political aspects of *Silex Scintillans, Part Two*.

The first relevant factor is the condition of Breconshire when he returned to it from military service either towards the end of 1645 or in the first part of 1646.[1] The crucial changes which began to occur in that year were both political and ecclesiastical, but it would appear that the religious discontent which ensued was the principal focus of popular attention:

Already Brecknockshire had had an opportunity to appreciate

[1] For different views concerning Vaughan's return from military service, see Hutchinson, op. cit., pp. 69–70.

that the growing power of Parliament meant the extension to the county of those arrangements for the reformation of religion which had been initiated in other parts of the kingdom. The two powerful Parliamentary committees known as the Committee for Scandalous Ministers and the Committee of Plundered Ministers were reviewing with a critical eye the work done by ministers of religion. Those who were deemed inefficient were being replaced by men who gave promise of preaching the Word of God more conscientiously. By 1649 Brecknockshire had seen this process at work. Seven clergymen had been ejected up to that year. They were Rowland Gwyn of Llangorse, Thomas Lewis of Llanfeygan, Josias Morgan of Vaynor, Thomas Powell of Cantreff, Rowland Watkins of Llanfrynach, Thomas Davis of Hay and Matthew Herbert of Llangattock, who had been six years tutor to Henry Vaughan the Silurist.[1]

There are two points of note here. The first is that five of the seven ministers must have been known to the Vaughan family as these churches are within a few miles of Llansantffraed. With one of them, Matthew Herbert, there was of course a closer connection, and it would be remarkable, also, if they did not know the incumbent at Hay, though it is rather further away than the others. It is very significant that such a high proportion of churchmen who were thrown out of their livings came from such a small part of this large county in which Vaughan himself lived. Secondly, it is clear that these ejections had been thoroughly discussed in Puritan circles for more than a year. The local churches round Vaughan's home must therefore have been fully aware of the impending catastrophe throughout 1648, as Vaughan was beginning work on the first part of *Silex Scintillans*.

This was by no means all. In August, 1647, Sir William Lewis of Llangorse, who sat in Parliament for Petersfield (Hants.), was one of eleven Presbyterians who were forced to withdraw from the House of Commons because they wished the army to be disbanded. But in fact Sir William, a very close neighbour of the Vaughans, was quite openly accused of protecting delinquents and of letting them off payment of fines. Vaughan's own immediate locality was therefore seen

[1] R. Tudor Jones, 'Religion in Post-Restoration Brecknockshire, 1660–1688', *Brycheiniog*, VIII (Brecknock Society, 1962), p. 12.

to be directly connected with the worst discontent and potential revolt.

The actual revolt, when it came in 1648, spread quickly through South Wales and developed into what is often termed the Second Civil War. Whether Vaughan had any direct part in it is not known; what is certain is that nobody in Breconshire could have been unaware of what was happening:

> Royalists were only too ready to exploit the revolt. In Brecon an attempt was made to garrison the town. But Colonel Thomas Horton who had been sent to prevent the troubles from spreading dispersed the Royalist sympathisers and arrested their leaders.[1]

By May 8th the revolt had been suppressed and the Puritan grip on the county inevitably tightened, with all the leaders either imprisoned or under threat. Only two months later Vaughan's brother, William, died and if we take the phrase 'dearest and nearest relatives' in 'The Mount of Olives' to refer to him, then it would certainly appear likely that his death is in some way connected with the violence of the Civil War. 1648 was therefore a most distressing year in every sense.[2] The only possible hope was that while the King lived there might be some chance, however small, of a rapprochement between the two bitterly divided camps. The execution of the King in January of the following year ended this hope and sealed the despair which had been mounting relentlessly ever since the end of the Civil War.

In view of all these events it is not in the least surprising that one of the major themes of the first part of *Silex Scintillans* is that of deliverance from bondage. The last six stanzas of 'Religion', the fourth poem in the book, proclaim this note strongly. Vaughan is centrally concerned here with the desperate need of an entire people for the Water of Life. True religion comes, like the water which sustains the bodies of men, from a secret, deep place, but in its long passage to the surface it has become tainted. As in so many of the poems in *Silex Scintillans* Vaughan deliberately combines different

[1] F. Rees, 'Breconshire during the Civil War', *Brycheiniog*, (Brecknock Society, 1962), p. 5.

[2] *Works*, p. 167, l.5. For a discussion of the cause of William's death see Hutchinson, op. cit., pp. 96–97.

Biblical passages in the thought and imagery. Here, quite apart from general allusions to the Psalms and Christ on the sea, there are two main sources. Christ's journey into Samaria is purposely combined with His attendance at the wedding feast in Cana of Galilee. Although he closes the poem with a very strong couplet based on the latter story, the central implied text is surely from the story of Christ and the woman of Samaria:

> Jesus answered and said unto her, Whosoever drinketh of this water shall thirst again:
> But whosoever drinketh of the water that I shall give him shall never thirst; but the water that I shall give him shall be in him a well of water springing up into everlasting life.
>
> (A.V., *John*, Ch. 4, vv.13–14.)

The underlying question is clear. What is the source of the corruption? It is important to recognize that Vaughan does not name man's own individual preference for sin, as Donne and Herbert had so often done, and as he himself did in many poems. Here is no individual aberration; it is nothing less than the spoiling of true religion by a whole corrupt regime. It is a picture of a people so starved of real spirituality that they mistake poison for the Water of Life. And only God, in Christ, as absolute Deliverer, can remedy this situation:

> So poison'd, breaks forth in some Clime,
> And at first sight doth many please,
> But drunk, is puddle, or meere slime
> And 'stead of Phisick, a disease;
>
> Just such a tainted sink we have
> Like that *Samaritans* dead *Well*,
> Nor must we for the Kernell crave
> Because most voices like the *shell*.
>
> Heale then these waters, Lord; or bring thy flock,
> Since these are troubled, to the springing rock,
> Looke downe great Master of the feast; O shine,
> And turn once more our *Water* into *Wine*!
>
> (p. 405, ll.41–52)

It is a cry repeated with less obvious power perhaps but

more poignancy three poems later in the very aptly titled poem 'The British Church'. The first line is interesting in that it could refer either to the King or Christ. The King was of course Head not only of the State but the Church too and the 'head' in the third line may well extend this reference to the King. If the King is indeed combined with Christ in a double meaning it would certainly add sharpness to the lament. But the central appeal of the poem is certainly addressed to Christ, for deliverance from a rude and ignorant military tyranny which is deriding even the central symbol of the Church's faith, the sacrificial offering of Christ Himself. There is no doubt that Vaughan uses this Puritan sacrilege as a general symbol of the destruction of the Church in the name of a new, and in his judgement, completely bogus religion:

Ah! he is fled!
And while these here their *mists*, and *shadows* hatch,
My glorious head
Doth on those hills of Mirrhe, and Incense watch.
Haste, hast my dear,
The Souldiers here,
Cast in their lots again,
That seamlesse coat
The Jews touch'd not,
These dare divide, and stain.

(p. 410, ll.1–10)

As in 'Religion' Vaughan's imagery is a combination of Biblical sources, in this instance the 'roe' and 'myrrh' of the *Song of Solomon* and the various gospel accounts of the Crucifixion. The meaning is clear. These Christian men and women have been slaughtered and the property of the Church destroyed or stolen. Nothing but the direct intervention of the Deliverer can save the people and their Church:

Write in thy bookes
My ravish'd looks
Slain flock, and pillag'd fleeces,
And hast thee so
As a young Roe
Upon the mounts of spices.

(p. 410, ll.15–20)

But Vaughan by no means confines himself to a general cry for deliverance from Puritan oppression. There are several poems in which he attacks specific Puritan abuses of the Church, its doctrine and its practice. In the reorganization of the Church, which we have already briefly discussed, it was inevitable that many Ministers, fearing the loss of their livings, collaborated with the authorities. Breconshire was certainly no exception. But staunch Royalists and Anglicans were bound to accuse them of responding to bribery. There is no doubt, either, that the Ministers who were ejected up to 1649 levelled the charge of corruption at the men who were to succeed them. This accusation would certainly seem to be present in several stanzas of 'Rules *and* Lessons':

> Through all thy *Actions*, *Counsels*, and *Discourse*,
> Let *Mildness*, and *Religion* guide thee out,
> If truth be thine, what needs a brutish force?
> But what's not *good*, and *just* ne'r go about.
> Wrong not thy Conscience for a rotten stick,
> That gain is dreadful, which makes spirits sick.
>
> To God, thy Countrie, and thy friend be true,
> If *Priest*, and *People* change, keep thou thy ground.
> Who sels Religion, is a *Judas Jew*,
> And, oathes once broke, the soul cannot be sound.
> The perjurer's a devil let loose: what can
> Tie up his hands, that dares mock God, and man?
>
> (p. 437, ll.37–48)

There were many local as well as national examples of 'brutish force' as Vaughan was writing. It is worth noting that Jenkin Jones of Llandetty, only a few miles from Vaughan's home, was both a fervent Puritan preacher and a most aggressive military commander, frequently cited by his opponents as a man who used physical threats and intimidation in order to change people's religious attitudes. 'Rotten stick' re-enforces the image of violence used in the service of untruth. His pointed accusation 'who sels Religion', in the context of '*Priest*, and *People* change', must be seen as a direct comment on the alleged inducements offered to ministers who were prepared to sympathize with the new order, and a number of ministers in Breconshire were certainly said to have done so. But in doing so they had violated their sacred oath of allegiance to the one true Church whose Head on Earth was the King. Hence 'oathes once broke', they had effectively sold their souls by this act of perjury.

Equally serious in Vaughan's view was the direct interference with the essential worship of the Church in celebration and sacrament. In 'Christ's Nativity', he is deeply aware of the damage being done to the Church, and the Christian souls it is supposed to protect, by the Puritan prohibition on the formal observation of the principal Christian Feasts, in this case the Nativity. The form of the poem is interesting. In a five stanza lyric of great beauty he uses first formal pastoral imagery and then more personal nature images to express the glory of the Saviour's birth and his own incapacity to respond to it as he should. There is only one reference to the responsibility of man in general:

> Man is their high-priest, and should rise
> To offer up the sacrifice.
>
> (p. 442, ll.11–12)

The implication is that man does not respond as he should.

In the second part, consisting of only eighteen lines, he develops this idea but changes the mood of the poem by making a direct thrust against the political masters who are deliberately preventing the response which every man should make:

> And shall we then no voices lift?
> Are mercy, and salvation
> Not worth our thanks? Is life a gift
> Of no more acceptation?
> Shal he that did come down from thence,
> And here for us was slain,
> Shal he be now cast off? no sense
> Of all his woes remain?
> Can neither Love, nor suff'rings bind?
> Are we all stone, and Earth?
> Neither his bloudy passions mind,
> Nor one day blesse his birth?
> Alas, my God! Thy birth now here
> Must not be numbred in the year.
>
> (p. 443, ll.5–18)

By including 'suff'rings' and 'bloudy passions' he not only reminds his readers that the Nativity and the Passion are inextricably linked in the worship of the Church, but he also points to the fact that Good Friday has been banned as a day of formal observation.

The structure of 'Christ's Nativity' is worthy of note because it gives us the overall pattern which he uses in most of the religious poems in which he is also making political attacks. God's love for man is shown in the birth of Christ. This is the formal statement in the first part of the poem and it is applied to the sin and therefore the necessity for grace in his own life. The particular sin and stubbornness of the men who claim to represent the new order is thus set quite firmly against the operation of the Divine Love. Vaughan is extremely careful not to indulge in political argument, weighing one course of action against another in terms of human strategy. He always attempts to show the extreme weakness and wickedness of the Puritan attitude to life by contrasting it sharply with Biblical truth and, where necessary, the established practice of the Church.

In 'Dressing' he attacks the Puritans for their violation of the Holy Communion. The prayer of longing for the Divine Presence, with which the poem opens, takes its main image from the *Song of Solomon* but its fervour and passion is more reminiscent of the *Book of Revelation*, which Vaughan used so often. However, the pattern is familiar in that God's sacred gift of the 'mysticall Communion' speaks to him, and should speak to man in general, of the essential character of God:

> Whatever thou dost bid, let faith make good,
> Bread for thy body, and Wine for thy blood.
> Give him (with pitty) love,
> Two flowres that grew with thee above;
> Love that shal not admit
> Anger for one short fit,
> And pitty of such a divine extent
> That may thy members, more than mine, resent.
> (p. 456, ll.23–30)

The central argument is that it should be impossible for man to refuse such pity and love. But as in 'Christ's Nativity'

Vaughan shows that some men do refuse. They know so little of God's goodness towards them that they insult His very Presence and his sacrificial offering by sitting down while they accept it:

> Give me, my God! thy grace,
> The beams, and brightness of thy face,
> That never like a beast
> I take thy sacred feast,
> Or the dread mysteries of thy blest bloud
> Use, with like Custome, as my Kitchin food.
> Some sit to thee, and eat
> Thy body as their Common meat,
> O let not me do so!
>
> (p. 456, ll.31–39)

At the end of the poem Vaughan implies that the Puritans have in fact lost all their reverence for God. His use of 'Saints' in the last line makes this absolutely clear; they were the self-styled saints who knew nothing of the Sainthood of God.

> Then kneel my soul, and body; kneel, and bow;
> If *Saints*, and *Angels* fal down, much more thou.
>
> (p. 456, ll.41–42)

There are two poems towards the end of the first part of *Silex Scintillans* in which Vaughan is concerned rather less with the alleged vandalism and hypocrisy of Puritan Church policy and more with the grievous condition of the entire nation. The first is 'The World', which will be discussed at greater length in the final section. But the political implications of the second stanza raise two interesting points. The first is that although Vaughan gives a complete and very powerful picture of the affairs of state, as distinct from Church dogma or administration, his 'darksome States-man' and all the problems which flow from his mismanagement, are seen under an aspect of eternity. Though Vaughan repeatedly condemns the Puritan regime for its interference with religious life it is important to recognize that he largely separates Church and State in his thinking. His statesman is judged, and found wanting, by the light of Divine truth as revealed in the *First Epistle of John*, (Ch 2, vv. 16–17) which he takes as his text, and also the *Book of Revelation* which inspires so much of the poem's thought and imagery. This statesman has chosen the darkness of death and destruction, rather than the light:

> The darksome States-man hung with weights and woe
> Like a thick midnight-fog mov'd there so slow
> He did nor stay, nor go:
> Condemning thoughts (like sad Ecclipses) scowl
> Upon his soul,
> And Clouds of crying witnesses without
> Pursued him with one shout.
> Yet dig'd the Mole, and lest his ways be found
> Workt under ground,
> Where he did Clutch his prey, but one did see
> That policie,
> Churches and altars fed him, Perjuries
> Were gnats and flies,
> It rain'd about him bloud and tears, but he
> Drank them as free.
>
> (pp. 466–7, ll.16–30)

The second question this stanza raises is whether Vaughan had any particular Puritan politician in mind. It is very tempting, of course, to identify the main figure with Cromwell, and there are certainly considerable similarities. But I would agree with Hutchinson that there is no real evidence for this view.[1] It would, in any case, be not only against the mood and spirit of the poem as a whole but at variance with Vaughan's practice of drawing a composite picture in order to illustrate a broad theme. This is his method throughout *Silex Scintillans*, with only one or two exceptions, and it is certainly the method he adopts here. The politician's inability to solve the nation's problems, his tendency to condemn and be negative, and his marked deviousness are general indications of what Vaughan believed about the nation's government at the time he was writing. Notwithstanding the pointed accusation that 'Churches and altars fed him' the point and force of this example of the world's decay and corruption is in its general reference and not in its identification with any particular person of the period.

[1] Hutchinson, op. cit., p. 121.

'The Constellation' is the other poem which is directly concerned with the condition of the state as a whole. It is very similar to 'The World' in that it seeks to place the greed and envy of the world, and more especially the sheer corruption and hypocrisy of Puritan politics, very firmly under the judgement of an Eternal Law. Indeed, this is even more pronounced in 'The Constellation' because of the description of man's restlessness and insecurity in a Universe of peace, calm and order. There seems no doubt that the Hermetic philosophy inspired some of the imagery and ideas here. The contrast is immediate and intensely dramatic, one of the most striking he ever achieved:

Some nights I see you in the gladsome East,
  Some others neer the West,
And when I cannot see, yet do you shine
  And beat about your endless line.

Silence, and light, and watchfulnes with you
  Attend and wind the Clue,
No sleep, nor sloth assailes you, but poor man
  Still either sleeps, or slips his span.

(p. 469, ll.9–16)

The move away from man in general to man under a vicious political regime is equally swift and Vaughan's picture is stark and particularized. In this it differs from 'The World' and most of his other poems in *Silex Scintillans*:

But here Commission'd by a black self-wil
  The sons the fathers kil,
The Children Chase the mother, and would heal
  The wounds they give, by crying, zeale.

Then Cast her bloud, and tears upon thy book
  Where they for fashion look,
And like that Lamb which had the Dragons voice
  Seem mild, but are known by their noise.

(p. 470, ll.37–44)

There is no doubt whatever that the King is 'the father' and the Church 'the mother'. But what is just as striking is the violence and terror which he depicts quite openly. After these two specific references he launches an attack which, as in 'The World', goes well beyond the area of organized religion. In both poems it is the entire corruption of the State which he takes as his theme, though he returns to the condition of the Church as an instrument of God's peace in the final stanza of 'The Constellation':

> Give to thy spouse her perfect, and pure dress,
> *Beauty* and *holiness*,
> And so repair these Rents, that men may see
> And say, *Where God is, all agree.*
>
> (p. 470, ll.57–60)

These two poems very near the end of the first part of *Silex Scintillans* would seem to signal a much more forthright attack on the Puritan regime than one sees earlier in his work. Vaughan was probably still shocked by the execution of the King. Furthermore the first batch of evictions of Church Ministers had by now been announced so his own locality would be reeling from a double blow. At least one thing was clear. All hope of a reconciliation between Parliamentarians and Royalists was now gone for some years. The general impact of this changed situation, coupled with his own anger and despair, certainly appears to have had its effect towards the end of his first volume. As he prepared these poems for publication and began work on others, the situation in Breconshire became even worse with the *Act for the Better Propagation and Preaching of the Gospel in Wales*, which was passed in February, 1650.

The evictions of 1649, to which reference has already been made, were in some respects a prelude to the Act of Propagation. What had been achieved by this change in ministers, and the consequent reorganization of their churches, would now, through the formal act, be possible on a much wider front and have a much more permanent basis. One needs, therefore, to note the main provisions of the Act and its chief propagandists before looking at the effects it had on Vaughan's own area.

> This Act, which was to be in force for three years, vested the control of the established Church in Wales in a body of 71 Commissioners. They were given authority to hear complaints against any Minister and if the allegations were substantiated by

the sworn evidence of witnesses and not disproved by the defendants, the Commissioners or any five of them had power to eject the offending minister and to allow up to one-fifth of the value of the living for the upkeep of his wife and children. Another body of 25 Approvers were named to examine the qualifications of men who were prepared to minister in the church, whether in the parishes or as itinerant preachers or as schoolmasters.[1]

It was unfortunate for the Anglican churches of Vaughan's own locality that two of the Approvers, men of extreme Puritan convictions and fiery temper, had an intimate knowledge of the churches near his home. One of them, Jenkin Jones of Llandetty, has already been mentioned. He was extremely active in the Tal-y-bont area, near to his home in Llandetty. The Act was carried out to the letter in all the churches he personally knew. The second Approver who would have been known to the Vaughan family was Vavasor Powell of Knucklas, who had been in trouble with the authorities for preaching extreme sermons as early as 1640, and was particularly active in the area which lay between Vaughan's home and the Olchon Valley. These two men of great power and undoubted courage were certainly detested by Anglicans and Royalists in the area and provoked great hostility by their claim that the Act of Propagation gave them virtually divine dispensation to order the life of the local churches as God had directly told them.

When the list of evictions was published as a consequence of the 1650 Act it was obvious that the churches in Vaughan's locality had suffered very badly:

> Richard Habberley, rector of Llys-wen, was charged with being a 'Common swearer, malignant and scandalous'. Illegal induction was the charge against both Griffith Hattley, vicar of Aberysgir, and Andrew Watkins, vicar of Penderyn, but John Perrot, rector of Cathedine, lost his living for being a common swearer and a drunkard and for helping the King in the war. Samuel Prytherch, rector of Llanhamlach, was ejected for drunkenness, fornication, lying and quarrelling and James Thomas, vicar of Llanwrthwl, for drunkenness, swearing and simony. Thomas Vaughan, vicar of Llansantffraed and brother of Henry Vaughan the Silurist,

[1] R. Tudor Jones, op. cit., p. 16.

> was described as a common swearer, no preacher and in arms against the Parliament.[1]

Of the twenty-five Ministers named, no fewer than thirteen had their churches within six miles of Vaughan's home, and every one of the churches within immediate walking distance of Llansantffraed are included. When these are coupled with the evictions of the previous year it can be seen that there must have been a wholesale disruption of religious practice in his locality. In addition the universal banning of the Book of Common Prayer, non-observance of Feast Days and suspension of Holy Communion imposed an almost intolerable strain on the loyalty of Anglicans. There must also have been acute personal distress at the discomfiture of so many clergymen who were well known in the area.

It is fortunate that the parish register of one Breconshire church has been preserved intact from this period. It is, of course, only one example and may well be an extreme case. Nevertheless it is important because the attitudes of strong Anglicans and Royalists in the county were very much shaped by what they heard of cases like this. The register is of Llanafan Fawr:

> After this time (sc. 1650) there was a generall cessation of officiating in Church either for Baptisme Marriadge or Buriall. The then Vicar William Wms Mr of Arts being ejected by the Act of Propagation of—49 & none officiated unless some curates did it in private houses or buried upon their perill in 1649 one Evan Bowen a mason by his trade & a souldier at ye Garrison of Red Castle by his profession being an illiterate man that could neither reade write or speake English was by the Commissioners made vicar of the parish who also did not at all officiate, nor could he tell how to Doe it. All that while the Church & Chapells belonging to Lanavanfawr, were without prayer or preaching or officiating unless in some of them some itinerants came once in a month or quarter or year in some not at all during that time or as yet in 1659 ...[2]

There is one further factor relevant to Vaughan's work in

[1] R. Tudor Jones, op. cit., pp. 18–19.

[2] A transcript in the hand of the late Principal, J. Morgan Jones of Bala-Bangor College, quoted in R. Tudor Jones, op. cit., p. 23.

the second part of *Silex Scintillans*. 1651 saw the beginning of a well organized movement of protest against the Act of Propagation. This affected South Wales as a whole but there were many signatures from Breconshire among the fifteen thousand on the Petition of Protest. This was presented to Parliament in March, 1652 and had been the subject of many meetings during which there was fierce denunciation of the Commissioners and the Approvers. Both Jenkin Jones and Vavasor Powell hit out angrily at their accusers and argued that their opponents' case was based on wild rumour and downright falsehood. The years in which Vaughan was completing his work were therefore filled with attack and counter-attack, protest, recrimination and bitter dispute, involving Church and community life which he must have known intimately.

There are some marked differences between the poems in Part One and those in Part Two. First, there are far more references to the Church politics of the age, and the tone of his comments is on the whole more bitter. One would expect no less in view of the marked deterioration in the situation. Second, his arguments against the violence of the Civil War, and against Puritanism in general, are developed more elaborately and at greater length. Finally, there is some attempt, particularly towards the end of the book, to gather together the many lines of his thought and reach a judgement upon which he can base his hopes and fears for the years that lie ahead.

The urgent note of Deliverance which we have noted in the first part of his work becomes even stronger in the second. It is sounded in the passage with which he chose to preface both parts of the work when he published it in 1655. It is therefore intended as a keynote to the work as a whole:

> O Lord, the hope of Israel, all they that forsake thee shall be ashamed; and they that depart from thee, shall be written in the earth, because they have forsaken the Lord, the fountain of living waters.
>
> (p. 393)

Vaughan does not use any one psalm but a skilful pastiche of various psalms to point his desperate need for release from his own slavery to sin, and also the wider captivity which the Puritan forces have imposed upon the land. But if Deliverance from the bondage of an alien religion is still his great cry he is more aware now that Judgement by God must be an integral part of that Deliverance.

There are several important poems in this second part of his work which link these two themes. The first is 'The Jews' in which he employs the general history of the Jewish people to show the folly and blindness of those who have turned away from God, refused to admit the love of Christ and have finally been judged by God. And the judgement is that they are to be shamed by the Gentiles so that all men may see what happens to those who will not respond to the promises of the Almighty:

> You were the *eldest* childe, and when
> Your stony hearts despised love,
> The *youngest*, ev'n the Gentiles then
> Were chear'd, your jealousie to move.
>
> Thus, Righteous Father! doest thou deal
> With Brutish men; Thy gifts go round
> By turns, and timely, and so heal
> The lost Son by the newly found.
>
> (p. 500, ll.42–49)

The change from the past to the present tense is unmistakable and the message is clear. The general comparison of the stubbornness of the Jews and the insensitivity and even downright wickedness of the Puritans cannot be escaped. But the poem is much more biting than that. Within the framework of his general comparison Vaughan has projected a powerful prophetic vision both of the deliverance of God and His Judgement. He uses the celebrated vision from the fourth chapter of the prophet Zechariah, but he simplifies the symbolism to some extent, using only the Angels and the Olive, not the gold candlestick and bowl. The effect is intended to be the same as in the vision of Zechariah, however. The deliverance, though long delayed, will come, angels will talk with men, Peace will renew the land and its people. All this is in the future, yet the promise of God is as sure as the branching of the Olive:

When the fair year
Of your deliverer comes,
And that long frost which now benums
Your hearts shall thaw; when Angels here
Shall yet to man appear,
And familiarly confer
Beneath the Oke and Juniper:
When the bright *Dove*
Which now these many, many Springs
Hath kept above,
Shall with spread wings
Descend, and living waters flow
To make drie dust, and dead trees grow;

O then that I
Might live, and see the Olive bear
Her proper branches! which now lie
Scattered each where,
And without root and sap decay
Cast by the husband-man away.

(p. 499, ll.1–19)

This poem is therefore not only a vision of peace and righteousness, but also a prophecy of Judgement. It is perhaps the symbol of the husband-man which finally gives it full penetration and power. The fulfilment of Zechariah's vision is worked out in the life of a corrupt society. The husband-men of *St. Matthew's Gospel* deliberately sought to deny the master what was rightfully his. They misused the estate and killed the master's servants and even the master's son but the end is swift and certain because the master 'will miserably destroy those wicked men, and will let out his vineyard unto other husbandmen, which shall render him the fruits in their seasons.' (A. V., *Matthew*, Ch. 21, vv.40–41). This is one of Vaughan's sharpest attacks on his Puritan masters, and also one of his most powerful poems. It also shows how short-sighted it is to attempt a separation of the political and the spiritual in his work. The force and clarity of his spiritual vision here springs from the bitter adversity of religious and political repression, and his emphasis on the Judgement of God arises from the conviction that before there is any lasting peace God must deal with the wickedness of the oppressors, and the righteous husband-men must at last become the custodians of God's estate.

There is no evidence whatever that Vaughan's appeal for judgement of the Puritan oppressors is diminished in the latter part of his work in *Silex Scintillans*, Part Two. It is true that he appears to become sickened by the blood that has been shed and he does recognize towards the end of his work that there must be reconciliation. Both these trends will be discussed later, but they in no way lessen his desire for God's justice upon the enemies of truth. In a remarkably fierce attack in 'The day of Judgement', one of the last poems in the collection and the second he wrote on this general theme, he catalogues the crimes of the new Puritan order. It is difficult to avoid the conclusion that he has in mind here the various malpractices which were alleged to have been committed under the umbrella of the Act of Propagation. He is in fact saying no more than was said in the Petition to Parliament of 1652, which has already been discussed. What is interesting, however, is that Vaughan believes the wickedness to have been so great that mercy, though it belongs to God, might be inappropriate. Perhaps there is only judgement left:

> Nor moan I onely (though profuse)
> Thy Creatures bondage and abuse;
> But what is highest sin and shame,
> The vile despight done to thy name;
> The forgeries, which impious wit
> And power force on Holy Writ,
> With all detestable designs
> That may dishonor those pure lines.
> O God! though mercy be in thee
> The greatest attribute we see,
> And the most needful for our sins;
> Yet, when thy mercy nothing wins
> But meer disdain, let not man say
> *Thy arm doth sleep*; but write this day
> Thy judging one: Descend, descend!
> Make all things new! and without end!
>
> (p. 531, ll.31–46)

There are two further points which arise from this passage. The first is that Vaughan does not separate personal sinning from political errors and misjudgements which lead to sin. The latter may be more deliberate and devilish than the former but he passes immediately from the one to the other. The crimes of a whole government are still manifestations of sin; political behaviour is after all an integral part of life. Secondly he ends the poem very characteristically with a call for newness of life. Nothing but the direct and full revelation of God's truth will save the nation from its sin and bitterness. The very great emphasis on the need for Divine Revelation throughout the whole of *Silex Scintillans* arises at least partly from his experience of the Puritan captivity.

There is evidence that the conflict between the demands of Vaughan's inner spiritual life and the public clamour of the world outside is much sharper in the second part of *Silex Scintillans* than it was in the earlier poems. Whereas in 'The World' and 'The Constellation' there is a degree of detachment and objectivity in the portrayal of the conflict, in two poems placed near the beginning of Part Two there are clear signs that he is having to defend his isolation, perhaps even for his own reassurance. These are 'White Sunday' and 'The Proffer'.

'White Sunday' is the third and final poem in a sequence exploring Ascension-Tide, which opens his second collection. Once again there appear to be clear echoes of the very recent hated legislation and its immediate consequences. The claim by the Puritan preachers, such as Jones and Powell, that only they could interpret God's commands to the people, not only upset but seriously demoralized Anglican congregations. Had the old Church gone for ever? Was this new dispensation what they must now believe? Moreover these same men proclaimed in their sermons that no days were special to them. Once saved, God's light shone on them from that moment through life and all eternity. The vehemence of Vaughan's cry against this blasphemy, coupled with the suggestion that at least he will protest while he still can, intensifies the sense of isolation conveyed in the lines:

> Can these new lights be like to those,
> These lights of Serpents like the Dove?
> Thou hadst no *gall*, ev'n for thy foes,
> And thy two wings were *Grief* and *Love*.

Though then some boast that fire each day,
And on Christs coat pin all their shreds;
Not sparing openly to say,
His candle shines upon their heads:

Yet while some rays of that great light
Shine here below within thy Book,
They never shall so blinde my sight
But I will know which way to look.

(p. 485, ll.9–20)

This feeling of extreme isolation deepens as the poem continues and the whole tragedy of the situation, sealed by the execution of the King and now brought home to ordinary people by the purge of the Church in 1649 and 1650, is conveyed with swiftness and power.

Again, if worst and worst implies
A State, that no redress admits,
Then from thy Cross unto these days
The *rule* without *Exception* fits.

(p. 485, ll.34–38)

'The Proffer' is an even starker poem than 'White Sunday' and the inner spiritual conflict is more intense. The spiritual quest he has undertaken seems threatened by worldly people who want to take all the goodness of his redeemed soul away. The sense of isolation which he portrayed in 'White Sunday' is considerably intensified, and the picture he gives us is of a soul under siege. His attackers want to destroy everything he has gained on his spiritual quest. Although he is passionate in defending the glories and joys that he has won with such difficulty there is a note of real desperation here:

Think you these longing eyes,
Though sick and spent,
And almost famish'd, ever will consent
To leave those skies,
That glass of souls and spirits, where well drest
They shine in white (like stars) and rest.

(p. 487, ll.19–24)

The 'poys'nous, subtile fowls' (l.13) who flock round him with their inducements are by no means all members of the Puritan regime. The conflict is not only with political forces but apparently with all those agencies which would dissipate his spiritual energy. But it is fairly easy to read into this poem all manner of mystical ideas for which there is little hard evidence. Durr takes this to very far lengths.[1] What is very definitely in the poem is a castigation of the Puritans who have corrupted the souls of so many, and are now trying to corrupt him. Hutchinson argues convincingly that it seems very likely Vaughan was offered some inducement under the Commonwealth, and that the middle sections of the poem constitute his answer.[2] It would not have been surprising if he had been approached to serve in some capacity. It is perfectly obvious from the history of Breconshire immediately following the Act of Propagation that the leading Puritans realized how isolated they were. They needed men to carry on the administration of the county; Vaughan's cousin, Charles Walbeoffe held office under them, though he was constantly in trouble for trying to temper their doctrine. Indeed, Vaughan's moving elegy, 'To the Pious Memory of C. W. Esquire', testifies to his courage in a period of great adversity.

The remarkable quality of 'The Proffer' is the sheer passion of the conflict. The contrast between the feebleness of his decaying life and the glory of eternity is rendered with a power and clarity which he rarely surpassed in all his work:

Shall my short hour, my inch,
My one poor sand,
And crum of life, now ready to disband
Revolt and flinch,
And having born the burthen all the day,
Now cast at night my Crown away?

No, No; I am not he,
Go seek elsewhere.
I skill not your fine tinsel, and false hair,
Your Sorcery
And smooth seducements: I'le not stuff my story
With your Commonwealth and glory.

(p. 487, ll.25–36)

[1] R. A. Durr, op. cit., pp. 100–111.
[2] Hutchinson, op. cit., p. 125.

'The Proffer' is arguably the most sombre poem he ever wrote, and his most scathing attack on the Commonwealth reveals an intensity and bitterness of mood which is a clear reflection both of the depression in Breconshire following the Act of Propagation and his own feeling of desolation and loneliness. Vaughan seems, in effect, to have reached a point of virtually complete exile, whether voluntary or not, from the political evil and social rottenness of the world about him.

The great prophetic notes of Deliverance and Judgement, begun in the first part of Vaughan's work, are carried right through the Second Part of *Silex Scintillans* and there they become deeper personal statements than earlier. There is another theme which becomes much more important in this second part, and that is his treatment of violence as an instrument of political policy. There is, in particular, a very significant group of poems placed in the latter half of the collection. In these he is tormented by the deaths which have been caused by the wilful shedding of blood.

The first in sequence is 'The Men of War', based upon the text in Luke's gospel:

> And Herod with his men of war set him at nought, and mocked and arrayed him in a gorgeous robe, and sent him again to Pilate.
>
> (A.V., *Luke*, Ch. 23, v. 11)

In fact Vaughan interprets the text broadly and takes it as a general base upon which to build his own defence against the violence of his age. There are three striking features of the poem which need comment. The first is his implication that the men who have so recently led a whole nation into bondage have in fact imprisoned themselves. This is the first time in *Silex Scintillans* that he has attacked the Puritans with the full moral weapons of Christian love and peace. The real text of the poem is therefore in the first few lines (A.V. *Revelation*, Ch. 13, v.10):

> *If any have an ear*
> Saith holy *John, then let him hear.*
> *He that into Captivity*
> *Leads others, shall a Captive be.*

Who with the sword doth others kill,
A sword shall his blood likewise spill.
Here is the patience of the Saints,
And the true faith, which never faints.

(p. 516, ll.1–8)

The second interesting feature is his quite open acknowledgement of the deep conflict between his desire to achieve power by force and the Christian commandment to use in his life the patience and love which alone can bring him his 'crown'. There seems no doubt that, whatever his views of Puritanism and the hypocrisy of its followers, he had been tempted to stifle his real views and feelings and accept an offer they either had made him or would make him.

Were not thy word (dear Lord!) my light,
How would I run to endless night,
And persecuting thee and thine,
Enact for *Saints* my self and mine.
But now enlighten'd thus by thee,
I dare not think such villainy;
Nor for a temporal self-end
Successful wickedness commend.

(p. 517, ll.9–16)

His deliberate use of 'Saints' here would seem to indicate who his tempters are, and later in the poem he prays for patience to 'slight the *Lure*' (l.40), which appears to have been an inducement from the Puritan 'saints' of his own home area.

The final point of interest is how powerfully he turns on himself, using the blood of the martyrs and finally the blood of Christ to show the moral depravity of the men of war who spill blood and finally drown in their own sin. It is a depravity so powerful that it threatened to engulf him. Only the blood of Christ makes it possible for him one day to enter the sainthood of God:

That when *thy Throne is set*, and all
These *Conquerors* before it fall,
I may be found (preserv'd by thee)
Amongst that chosen company,
Who by no blood (here) overcame

But the blood of the *blessed Lamb*.

(pp. 517–518, ll.47–52)

It seems clear from this poem that Vaughan could see no end to the shedding of blood if revenge became, as it certainly had become for some of his friends, a way of life and reason for being. Despite the extraordinary tensions and conflicts the poem reveals, Vaughan's final underlying message is that the bloodshed has to end if the nation wishes to return finally to sanity and peace under God.

'Abels blood', placed five poems later in the collection, reveals both the sadness and the passion for peace contained in 'The Men of War', but there is no further hint of any offer which the Puritans had made to him. It is more stark and dramatic than the earlier poem and the obsession with the shedding of blood is even greater. Starting with a brief but telling picture from *Genesis*, Vaughan emphasizes the sheer vileness of the taking of life. For him the most striking feature of the story is that Abel's voice is still heard crying to his Maker. The implication is that the soul of the murdered man has no final peace or rest:

Sad, purple well! whose bubling eye
Did first against a Murth'rer cry;
Whose streams still vocal, still complain
    Of bloody *Cain*,
And now at evening are as red
As in the morning when first shed.

(p. 523, ll.1–6)

What follows is interesting in two respects. First, the way in which Vaughan constructs a complex and powerful web of images on the parallel of water and blood, translating his general argument into a particular indictment of the bloody crimes committed in the Civil War and after. It is perhaps the most frightening picture in all his poetry. Those who have died would seem to have found no peace in death, nor can they ever find peace until God, as righteous Judge, has avenged their deaths. So the souls of the righteous slain move, as if in Purgatory, restless and unfulfilled, and Vaughan's specific use of 'altar' (l.20) would seem to symbolize that cause for which they died. The new men of religion, guilty of so many murders, have abolished the altar from their worship, mocking God's Sanctuary just as they have mocked God's great commandment. This is also one of the many occasions in *Silex Scintillans* in which Vaughan cleverly adapts a Biblical passage to his own direct purpose and uses it to emphasize a deep and burning grievance which shows plainly all his bitterness against the Parliamentarians and the terrible wrongs of the Puritans. The passage upon which lines 20–22 of his poem are based is taken from one of Vaughan's favourite books, *Revelation*:

> And when he had opened the fifth seal, I saw under the altar the souls of them that were slain for the word of God, and for the testimony which they held:
> And they cried with a loud voice, saying, How long, O Lord, how long and true, dost thou not judge and avenge our blood on them that dwell on the earth.
> (A.V., *Revelation*, Ch. 6, vv. 9–10)

It is an exceptionally vivid and dramatic use of the Bible to underline his theme.

> What thunders shall those men arraign
> Who cannot count those they have slain,
> Who bath not in a shallow flood,
> But in a deep, wide sea of blood?
> A sea, whose lowd waves cannot sleep,
> But *Deep* still calleth unto *deep*:
> Whose urgent *sound* like unto that
> *Of many waters*, beateth at
> The everlasting doors above,
> Where souls behinde the altar move,
> And with one strong, incessant cry
> Inquire *How long?* of the most high.
> (pp. 523–4, ll.11–22)

The second interesting feature is that in the passage which immediately follows he makes a direct reference to himself, thanking God for having kept him from 'bloody men' (l.29) when he was in 'thick death and night!' (l.32). It is the only direct mention in *Silex Scintillans* of his own immediate involvement in the violence of the Civil War. But in the passage which closes the poem he prays passionately for those who have been slain. One wonders whether his reference to 'That proudly spilt and despis'd blood' is not a specific reminder of the King's death. There may also be an intentional comparison between the King and Christ in the final couplet, which would point even more forcibly his savage denunciation of the Puritan oppressors, and his prayer that the souls of all the martyrs shall find peace:[1]

> I, may that flood,
> That proudly spilt and despis'd blood,
> Speechless and calm, as Infants sleep!
> Or if it watch, forgive and weep
> For those that spilt it! May no cries
> From the low earth to high Heaven rise,
> But what (like his, whose blood peace brings)
> Shall (when they rise) *speak better things*,
> Then *Abels* doth! may *Abel* be
> Still single heard, while these agree
> With his milde blood in voice and will,
> *Who* pray'd for those that did him kill!
>
> (p. 524, ll.33–44)

'Abels blood' is a poem of quite extraordinary power and beauty, which completely contradicts the assertion that Vaughan's finest poetry has nothing to do with the political tumult of his time.

In the very next poem of the collection, 'Righteousness', Vaughan again deals with the shedding of blood. The righteous man has 'The clean, pure hand, which never medled pitch?' (l.10), and in the sixth stanza he gives a composite picture reflecting once more the agony and bitterness of the Civil War and the troubled violent years since:

> Who spills no blood, nor spreds
> Thorns in the beds
> Of the distrest, hasting their overthrow;
> Making the time they had
> Bitter and sad
> Like *Chronic* pains, which surely kill, though slow
>
> (p. 525, ll.25–30)

[1] Some of the extreme supporters of Charles I did see in his death a parallel with the death of Christ. See C. V. Wedgwood, *The Trial of Charles I* (London, 1964), pp. 235–236.

There were certainly numerous cases in Breconshire, as elsewhere, of harassment of men who had the wrong political and religious colours, but Vaughan's picture here might well include the death of William two years after the end of the Civil War, to which reference has already been made. Certainly 'Chronic' would seem to indicate long and slow torment.

Vaughan's persistent conflict between the desire for revenge and the need to reach true peace of spirit may well be said to reach a climax in 'Jacobs Pillow, and Pillar', in which he devotes a substantial part of his poem to an exploration of the vicarious suffering of Christ. Once again he is forced to place this example of Christ in the context of his own age and now he seems to reach a resolution of his conflict. It is only the heart which knows and practises God's peace which can resist the advance of evil and wait in patience until God brings about complete deliverance.

> .... And when slain by the crowd
> (Under that stately and mysterious cloud
> Which his death scatter'd) he foretold the place,
> And form to serve him in, should be true grace
> And the meek heart, not in a Mount, nor at
> *Jerusalem*, with blood of beasts, and fat.
> A heart is that dread place, that awful Cell,
> That secret Ark, where the milde Dove doth dwell
> When the proud waters rage: when Heathens rule
> By Gods permission, and man turns a Mule.
> This little *Goshen*, in the midst of night,
> And Satans seat, in all her Coasts hath light,
>
> (pp. 527–8, ll.21–32)

Is there, by the end of his work in *Silex Scintillans*, any substantial change in his attitude towards the Puritan rulers, their supporters, propagandists and preachers? There is certainly no alteration whatever in his view that their purposes are wrongly conceived and that Puritanism in his own part of the world had been as disastrous in practice as the theory and dogma would have led him to believe. Although there are fewer detailed references to the abuse of the Church in the last half of Part Two than there are in the rest of his work, there is no clear evidence that he has changed his viewpoint. He condemns both the method and substance of the new regime right to the end. Indeed his attack on their beliefs and the consequences of those beliefs is both sharper and deeper towards the end of his work than at the beginning. But there is also, towards the end of the collection, a realization that there must be a new initiative if the worst of the rancour and bitterness is to be cleared away. The emphasis on the need for peace in 'Jacobs Pillow, and Pillar' reveals only one aspect of this shift of emphasis. Several of the last poems stress the Christian qualities of mercy, forgiveness and fresh hope. In 'The Feast' he rejoices in a newness of life and thanks God for 'This healing peace' (p. 535, l.56). In both 'Tears' and 'The Throne' he prays for true humility of life and a quiet obedience to the will of God. Coming after the blood-guilt poems in sequence, these late poems re-enforce the impression that he was utterly weary of the violence of past years.

Finally, in 'L'Envoy' which closes his book and is therefore of particular importance, there is absolutely no doubt that he wants the great process of healing to begin quickly. But he is still insistent that this cannot mean peace on any terms. The men who have done wrong must face the judgement of God, but once that has happened there must be a general movement towards real peace. It may well be that two general factors influenced Vaughan's work as he reached a conclusion. First, the undoubted success of the campaign to amend the Act of Propagation. The impassioned protest against the bill and the inability of Jenkin Jones and others to suppress the protestors undoubtedly made for a resurgence of confidence among many Anglicans and supporters of the old order. The Act was not renewed in 1653, so the protestors could claim victory. The other factor of importance may have been the ending of the hated Long Parliament in 1653 and the beginning of the Protectorate. There was some ground for hope that the coming years would be more stable and at least put an end to the worst of the petty tyranny.

In 'L'Envoy', therefore, Vaughan is able to pass fairly quickly and naturally from Judgement, to Mercy and Reconciliation:

Frustrate those cancerous, close arts
Which cause solution in all parts,
And strike them dumb, who for meer words
Wound thy beloved, more then swords.
Dear Lord, do this! and then let grace
Descend, and hallow all the place.
Incline each hard heart to do good,
And cement us with thy sons blood,
That like true sheep, all in one fold
We may be fed, and one minde hold.
(pp. 542–3, ll.39–48)

This final poem is an excellent example of the way in which the sorrows and losses of the Civil War, and its deeply troubled aftermath, have deepened and intensified Vaughan's own spiritual awareness. 'L'Envoy' is a complete answer to those critics who have attempted to separate the political and public aspects of his poetry from his personal quest for the certainty and sublimity of God's truth, and so depict him as a man who retreats into an inner Kingdom. This is to misunderstand the entire basis of his poetry. There are certainly occasions when he longs for an escape from the particular troubles and dangers of his times; it would be very strange if he had not done so. There are also moments when he allows his detestation of the Puritans to overwhelm his judgement so that he tends to become purely propagandist, but these moments are rare. The quality of most of the poems which treat the political and religious issues of his period is very high, and there is a depth and consistency in both the imagery and thought of the best of them which is very impressive. Poems such as 'Religion', 'The Constellation', 'The Proffer', 'The Jews', 'The Men of War', 'Abels blood', 'Jacobs Pillow, and Pillar' and 'L'Envoy' should be included in any selection of the finest poetry he wrote. They would give a much more balanced view of Vaughan's work in *Silex Scintillans* than anthologies usually do. They would also help to explain, at least in part, the anguish of 'the captivity' which substantially affects his distinctive vision of life.

Therefore write in their hearts thy law,
And let these long, sharp judgements aw
Their very thoughts, that by their clear

And holy lives, mercy may here
Sit regent yet, and blessings flow
As fast, as persecutions now.
So shall we know in war and peace
Thy service to be our sole ease,
With prostrate souls adoring thee,
Who turn'd our sad captivity!

(p. 543, ll. 53–62)

II

'BLEST INFANT BUD'

The significance of Infant innocence in Vaughan's poetry has long been acknowledged by serious students of his work. But strangely there has been only scant appreciation of the central influence of the Bible on his treatment of the child. Certainly there are strong elements of both Hermeticism and Platonism in his vision of the child, but the influences in no way compare with the Bible, and especially the New Testament, as the dominant source of his thought and imagery. It is our purpose in this chapter to examine in detail the theme of the innocence of the child and childhood in his religious poetry, and to place it directly in the context of his belief as an Anglican and his own personal vision of Biblical truth.

To take the full measure of Vaughan's treatment of the child it is necessary first of all to state in brief outline what were the main tenets of Anglican belief regarding the new-born child at the time Vaughan was writing *Silex Scintillans*. There is no doubt whatever of the dominance in the Anglican thought of the Thirty-Nine Articles of Religion of 1652. The Twenty-Seventh Article, *Of Baptism* does, of course, deal quite directly with the new-born child:

> Baptism is not only a sign of profession, and mark of difference, whereby Christian men are discerned from others that be not christened, but it is also a sign of Regeneration or new Birth, whereby, as by an instrument, they that receive Baptism rightly are grafted into the Church; the promises of forgiveness of sin, and of our adoption to be the sons of God by the Holy Ghost, are visibly signed and sealed; Faith is confirmed, and Grace increased by virtue of prayer unto God. The Baptism of young Children is in any wise to be retained in the Church, as most agreeable with the institution of Christ.

The implication is therefore clear. Those who are not baptised are not of Christ. Further, if baptism signifies 'new Birth' then the natural birth of the child into the world is not at all sufficient to rid us of sin.

And yet the Church has by no means spoken with one

mind on this crucial matter. For several centuries after the death of Christ there had been no fixed belief in the absolute necessity for Baptism as a means of saving the soul from damnation. However, the issue did become acute for the mediaeval Church Fathers, who became convinced that without baptism the child remained in sin:

> What sin could they be guilty of which would have to be forgiven? From Cyprian of Antioch came the answer: the sin of Adam. Arguing from the words of scripture (*Romans* 5:12–21) and the practice of the church, Cyprian contended that baptism washed away the guilt contracted by the human race in Adam's fall, and that this was why the church encouraged parents to baptize their infants.[1]

This view was re-enforced and developed by Augustine a century and a half later. But it was not accepted by all Churchmen. Most notably the British monk, Pelagius, questioned the whole basis of the doctrine, and the grounds of his objection are extremely important because they foreshadow the very doubts and contradictions one notes in the sixteenth and seventeenth centuries:

> Pelagius believed that people were born in a state of 'original grace' which was the reason for their natural goodness, and that what was lost by Adam was not this grace but a further grace, a 'grace of pardon' which was won by Christ and received by sinful adults when they were baptised. Children of course were born innocent and so had no need of baptism.[2]

In his treatise *On the Acquisition and Remission of Sins* Augustine gave his classic reply to this heresy of Pelagius, asserting that sin was in the soul from the moment of birth and could only be removed by the formal act of baptism:

> Why would it be necessary to form the little child in a figure of Christ's death through baptism if it were not already poisoned by the serpent's bite?[3]

Augustine's view prevailed and has, in fact, coloured the

[1] J. Martos, *Doors to the Sacred, A Historical Introduction to the Sacraments in the Christian Church*, S.C.M. Press, (London, 1981), p. 173.
[2] J. Martos, op. cit., pp. 174–5.
[3] J. Martos, op. cit., p. 176.

entire thinking of many branches of the Christian Church until quite recent times. And yet this belief in original sin has never been wholeheartedly accepted by all leading Churchmen. The further one looks into Church history and theological belief the more ambiguity one finds on this question of the child's nature and status. Within the Anglican doctrine of Vaughan's own lifetime, indeed, one can find traces of the two views on this question.

Jeremy Taylor, in *The Great Exemplar, The History of the Life and Death of the Holy Jesus*, restates for the Anglicans of his own day the doctrine of original sin and its consequences for the Christian and the Church:

> In Baptism we are born again; and this infants need in the present circumstances and for the same great reason that men of age and reason do. For our natural birth is either of itself insufficient, or is made so by the Fall of Adam and the consequent evils, that nature alone, or our first birth, cannot bring us to Heaven, which is a supernatural end, – if nature cannot bring us to Heaven, grace must, or we can never get thither; if the first birth cannot, a second must.[1]

But in 1655 Taylor published *Unum Necessarium or The Doctrine and Practice of Repentance*. This treatise was stongly condemned by many in the Church because Taylor appeared to call in question the accepted doctrine of Original Sin. He argued strongly that it was not sin at all in the proper sense of the word. One passage in the treatise is especially relevant to our consideration of Vaughan's treatment of the child. Recalling Seneca's dictum that 'nature does not engage us upon vice but leaves us free', Taylor continues:

> But we make ourselves prisoners and slaves by vicious habits; or, as St. Cyril expresses it ... 'We came into the world without sin,' meaning, without sin properly so called, 'but now we sin by choice, and by election bring a kind of necessity upon us.'[2]

A little later in his argument Taylor asserts that 'it is almost by

[1] More and Cross, *Anglicanism, The Thought and Practice of the Church of England Illustrated from the Religious Literature of the Seventeenth Century*, S.P.C.K., (London, 1935), p. 428.

[2] More and Cross, op. cit., pp. 651–2.

all men acknowledged to be unjust that infants should be eternally tormented in the flames of hell for original sin . . .'[1]

There is no doubt whatever that the importance of Baptism in the life of the seventeenth-century Anglican Church would not have been lost upon Vaughan. Time and again, as has been shown already, he asserts in his poetry the virtues of traditional Anglican piety and the value of the Sacraments, and defends them from Puritan attack. But Taylor's view, written at virtually the same time as *Silex Scintillans*, and recalling as it does the much earlier and more liberal doctrine of the Church's early Fathers, represented a strong minority view within Anglicanism, of which Vaughan could not have been unaware.

In Vaughan's own experience, however, this great doctrinal issue could not be finally settled one way or the other by theologians. It was the whole essence of his religious experience that he tested the validity of his spiritual convictions by the Word of God itself. Though he was loyal to his own Anglican traditions, it is difficult to escape the conclusion that the final authority for all he believed rested squarely upon the Word of God. And in his poems which treat the Child or Childhood he is clearly aware of all the main Biblical texts, and especially those in the New Testament. The one basic text which seems to underpin his whole vision of the Child is the one reported by Matthew, but rendered with only slight variations by both Mark and Luke:

> At the same time came the disciples unto Jesus, saying, Who is the greatest in the Kingdom of Heaven?
>
> And Jesus called a little child unto him, and set him in the midst of them,
>
> And said, Verily I say unto you, Except ye be converted, and become as little children, ye shall not enter into the Kingdom of Heaven.
>
> Whosoever therefore shall humble himself as this little child, the same is greatest in the Kingdom of Heaven.
>
> And whoso shall receive one such little child in my name receiveth me.
>
> But whoso shall offend one of these little ones which believe

[1] More and Cross, op. cit., p. 652.

in me, it were better for him that a millstone were hanged about his neck, and that he were drowned in the depth of the sea.

(A.V., *Matthew*, Ch. 18, vv.1–6)

The deliberate contrast between the sinful adult world, and the innocence of the small child, the demand that men and women shall be converted back to the purity of the original state of grace (the very opposite of the doctrine of Original Sin) and the clear implication that the humility of the little child shall be a necessary pre-condition for entry into God's Kingdom so that they shall be able to respond instinctively to the call of God, are all quite centrally contained in Vaughan's poetry of childhood and all three priorities will emerge as one studies the poems in detail.

Vaughan's poetry of childhood may conveniently be separated into three general areas. There are firstly those poems in which he treats childhood as a state very much apart from the rest of mortal experience, a haven and refuge to which the soul looks back and recognizes the purity and innocence from which we came. Poems such as 'The Retreate', 'The Buriall of an Infant' and 'Child-hood', which belong to this group, may be considered major expositions of childhood as a state far removed from original sin, rather as a state of original grace.

In the second group of poems he refers to childhood more briefly, sometimes only by general implication. Nevertheless the picture he draws is interesting and compelling. It is that of the young child's instinctive response to God, and is usually given as an illustration of the spontaneous insight into the nature and holiness of God which all people need but so conspicuously lack.

Finally there is a small group of poems, all in the second part of *Silex Scintillans*, in which infancy (whether of human or animal) becomes a symbol of humility, meekness and true peace without which no full spiritual life is possible. And these poems accompany the plea for regeneration and reconciliation in the life of both individual and nation which has already been observed in his work.

In looking at these three groups of poems the individual poems will be taken in the order they appear in *Silex Scintillans* because there does seem to be a significant development of his views and there are also some important differences between the two parts of his work.

The first poem in *Silex Scintillans* in which childhood is used substantially, and as an important part of the poem's main theme, is 'Isaac's Marriage'. Basing his poem on the 'Genesis' narrative in which Isaac prays as a preparation for his marriage, Vaughan explores in depth the relationship between the bridegroom and the young child (See A.V., *Genesis*, Ch. 24, vv.61–67). One striking and complex picture is central to the entire poem because it gives us the instinctive response of the young child to the call of God:

> But thou a Chosen sacrifice wert given,
> And offer'd up so early unto heaven
> Thy flames could not be out; Religion was
> Ray'd into thee, like beams into a glasse,
> Where, as thou grewst, it multipli'd and shin'd
> The sacred Constellation of thy mind.
>
> (p. 408, ll.5–10)

The central statement of the poem is therefore of the complete innocence and obedience of the young child, and though the sacrifice demanded of Abraham by God is not in the end exacted, the special nature of what happens to Isaac as a child means that he is designated as a servant of God from that moment of his life. It is impossible for the holy flames of his life to be put out.

The devotion of his father and his own innocent complicity were so intense that they were greater than the fire which could be lit from wood collected for the burnt offering; the spiritual fire in his life could never be put out.

Three distinct themes emerge from this central statement. The first is one which contains a sharper edge of contemporary social observation and comment than in most of his lyrics. It is a view of child innocence and artlessness, contrasted directly with the artifice and contrivance of Vaughan's own age. Isaac never lost in his soul the simplicity of the child, but as Vaughan looks around him at his own social conventions he observes that this simplicity has gone, and in its place is a wild and blasphemous excess:

> . . . . Hadst thou but the art

Of these our dayes, thou couldst have coyn'd thee twenty
New sev'ral oathes, and Complements (too) plenty;
O sad, and wilde excesse! and happy those
White dayes, that durst no impious mirth expose!
When Conscience by lew'd use had not lost sense,
Nor bold-fac'd custome banish'd Innocence;
Thou hadst no pompous train, nor *Antick* crowd
Of young, gay swearers, with their needlesse, lowd
Retinue; All was here smooth as thy bride
And calm like her, or that mild Evening-tide;

(p. 408, ll.14–24)

The holiness of 'white days' is directly contrasted with the 'wilde excesse' which is far removed from innocence; the picture of Conscience, the sure guide of the soul, is one which Vaughan develops further in 'The Retreate'.[1] This passage implies strongly that 'bold-fac'd custome' has inevitably robbed life of its original innocence, except in the lives of the few exceptional men and women who were dedicated by God.

The second theme is that of the holiness of infant life, attended by something of God's own majesty. Isaac, unlike other young children, has never lost this holiness and majesty so that in him, as a fully grown young man, we are able to see something of the splendour and simplicity of the original innocence. And then in a passage of striking beauty and power Vaughan transfers some of Isaac's qualities to his bride:

Yet, hadst thou nobler guests: Angels did wind
And rove about thee, guardians of thy minde,
These fetch'd thee home thy bride, and all the way
Advis'd thy servant what to do, and say;
These taught him at the *well*, and thither brought
The Chast, and lovely object of thy thought;
But here was ne'r a Complement, not one
Spruce, supple cringe, or study'd look put on,
All was plain, modest truth: Nor did she come
In *rowles* and *Curles*, mincing and stately dumb,
But in a Virgins native blush and fears
Fresh as those roses, which the day-spring wears.
O sweet, divine simplicity!

(p. 408, ll.25–37)

[1] See p. 419, ll.15–16.

'Virgin', 'fresh', 'sweet' and 'simplicity' are all terms Vaughan will use many times in his vision of childhood, and they are made richer here by being seen as part of the vision of Elizabeth and Zacharias as they thank God for the 'day-spring from on high' and look forward to the birth of their child (A.V., *Luke*, Ch. 1, v.78).

The third and final theme is Isaac's complete dependence upon God and upon his father Abraham, God's special servant. The divine innocence of childhood which still surrounds him gives him easy access to God, so that he is able to leave the world in which he lives and speak directly to God. In several passages towards the end of this long and complex lyric Vaughan seems to imply that the innocence born of childhood, and never lost to the true saints, can make possible those direct flights to God's eternity, which are vital for the refreshment of the soul:

> And now thou knewest her coming, It was time
> To get thee wings on, and devoutly climbe
> Unto thy God, for Marriage of all states
> Makes most unhappy, or most fortunates;
> This brought thee forth, where now thou didst undress
> Thy soul, and with new pinions refresh
> Her wearied wings, which so restor'd did flye
> Above the stars, a track unknown, and high,
> And in her piercing flight perfum'd the ayer
> Scatt'ring the *Myrrhe*, and incense of thy pray'r.
>
> (p. 409, ll.43–52)

The final passage of the poem shows how child innocence fore-shadowed the experience of age. The young child was already a Father of the Church, and had it within him to become the saint. It is a passage very reminiscent of one of Vaughan's most moving secular poems: 'An Epitaph upon the Lady *Elizabeth*, Second Daughter to his late Majesty', especially in the passage which contrasts the King's experience in facing sufferings and tribulations with his daughter's innocence and inexperience in a ruthless and cruel world:

> Others, e're their afflictions grow,
> Are tim'd, and season'd for the blow,

But thine, as *Rhumes* the tend'rest part,
Fell on a *young* and *harmless* heart.

(p. 63, ll.19–22)

Isaac is also without experience but such is the quality of his childhood that he is completely superior in Christian grace:

Others were tym'd, and train'd up to't but thou
Diddst thy swift yeers in piety out-grow,
Age made them rev'rend, and a snowie head,
But thou wert so, e're time his snow could shed;
Then, who would truly limne thee out, must paint
First, a *young Patriarch*, then a *marri'd Saint*.

(p. 410, ll.67–72)

There are so many ideas and images of the special nature and status of Childhood in 'Isaac's Marriage' that it must be regarded as a quarry which he used freely in later poems. It gave him an opportunity to try out so many arguments. It also linked the sublimity of childhood with direct Biblical story and text, and thus established a mode which is of tremendous importance in Vaughan's treatment of childhood as a whole.

In 'Mans fall, and Recovery', the picture of childhood takes only a few lines but is very telling in its effect. The poem is based directly on a verse in the fifth chapter of 'Romans' which speaks of the sin of Adam, cancelled out only by the righteousness of Christ.[1] Vaughan depicts himself, the adult man, as a 'sully'd flowre' of God. His imagery is dramatic and the arresting opening of the poem would seem to imply that he is cut off completely from the joy he has once known:

[1] Vaughan's usual practice is to quote the verse from the Authorized Version. In this case, however, he gives his own gloss on the version. The verse in A.V. is: 'Therefore as by the offence of one judgement came upon all men to condemnation; even so by the righteousness of one the free gift came upon all men unto justification of life.' Vaughan varies it thus: 'As by the offence of one, the fault came in all men to condemnation, so by the righteousness of one, the benefit abounded towards all men to the justification of life.' The verse is also wrongly referenced in Vaughan's text as *Romans*, Ch. 18, v.19. There is, of course, no eighteenth chapter of Romans. The verse is verse 18, and is from chapter 5.

Farewell you Everlasting hills! I'm Cast
Here under Clouds, where stormes, and tempests blast
    This sully'd flowre
Rob'd of your Calme, nor can I ever make
Transplanted thus, one leafe of his t'awake,
(p. 411, ll.1–5)

The state of the blessedness he knew in early childhood is immediately contrasted with the world he has sunk to now, in which he is 'a slave to passions'. That original state is characterized quickly but clearly. It was first a world in which he was aware of the majesty of God. Though he was not specifically dedicated like Isaac, Vaughan's deliberate use of 'train' (l.10) makes clear that he could well appreciate the awe of God. It is normally used in the Old Testament to denote great majesty, as in the famous vision of Isaiah when he saw 'the Lord sitting upon a throne, high and lifted up, and his train filled the temple' (A.V., *Isaiah*, Ch. 6, v.1).

But it was a world in which Vaughan was aware of 'lights' and as if to re-enforce the brightness of his vision he calls them 'Sun-shine dayes'. The image is similar to many Biblical pictures which portray Paradise as cloudless. But in speaking of 'lights' rather than light in general and designating them as 'sure guides' he is clearly identifying the world of childhood as one in which the soul responded instinctively in every way to the glory of the Creator, so that this world was one of full knowledge; the picture is not only Biblical, but Platonic also. And as if to under-score the point Vaughan contrasts all this with the world as he knows it now, in which only one instinct is left, and that is conscience.

    Besides I've lost
A traine of lights, which in those Sun-shine dayes
Were my sure guides, and only with me stayes
    (Unto my cost,)
One sullen beame, whose charge is to dispense
More punishment, than knowledge to my sense;
(pp. 411–12, ll.9–14)

But Vaughan's picture is not only of himself. He makes it perfectly clear that he is taking man in every age and clime as his subject:

Two thousand yeares
I sojourn'd thus; at last *Jeshuruns* king
Those famous tables did from *Sinai* bring;
These swell'd my feares,
Guilts, trespasses, and all this Inward Awe,
(p. 412, ll.15–19)

Here is a picture of man completely lacking in righteousness, and Vaughan's deliberate designation of the people of Israel as Jeshurun's, the people of righteousness, as declared in '*Deuteronomy*', forces home the point that man, robbed of the innocence and glory of childhood, and separated also from the righteous people of God who walked by faith, can only be saved by the blood of Christ. In the last few lines he emphasizes again, as he has done in the earlier parts of the poem, his personal need for this salvation, and by referring directly to the 'fathers journeys' he declares that he is now able to join the ancient patriarchs of the Church in the waters of righteousness. The exact point he is making here is the one contained in the celebrated eleventh chapter of the '*Epistle to the Hebrews*': the promise of Christ, enabling the latter generations to enter into the full faith of the people of God, without the long experience of pain and travail which the Fathers had to endure. And the implication of the poem as a whole is that this same promise is able to give to him, sullied by sin, at least something of the original glory he knew as a child:

His saving wound
Wept bloud, that broke this Adamant, and gave
To sinners Confidence, life to the grave;
This makes me span
My fathers journeys, and in one faire step
O're all their pilgrimage, and labours leap,
For God (made man,)
Reduc'd th' Extent of works of faith; so made
Of their *Red Sea*, a *Spring*; I wash, they wade.
(p. 412, ll.24–32)

Vaughan returns to the theme of a glory that has been lost, in one of the poems in the first part of his work which is marked only with a paragraph-mark for a heading. This is 'Thou that know'st for whom I mourne', a most moving elegy, and one of several which Vaughan may well have written in memory of his brother, William. There are three interesting features of the elegy.

First, he has linked smallness and frailty, which is normally associated with the tiny infant, with the world of inanimate Nature. He does, of course, very frequently praise Nature for its instinctive response to its Creator. But here the main idea is that the smallest shall become the greatest, the same principle which Christ applied to the life of the small child:

> And Jesus, perceiving the thought of their heart, took a child, and set him by him, and said unto them, Whosoever shall receive this child in my name, receiveth me: for he that is least among you, the same shall be great.
>
> (A.V., *Luke*, Ch. 9, vv.47–48)

Vaughan achieves his effect by contrasting the huge labour needed to produce a sensitive man with the tiniest, most fragile elements of God's creation.

> Nine months thy hands are fashioning us,
> And many yeares (alas!)
> E're we can lisp, or ought discusse
> Concerning thee, must passe;
> Yet have I knowne thy slightest things
> A *feather*, or a *shell*,
> a *stick*, or *Rod* which some Chance brings
> The best of us excell,
> Yea, I have knowne these shreds out last
> A faire-compacted frame
> And for one *Twenty* we have past
> Almost outlive our name.
>
> (p. 417, ll.17–28)

The second feature of interest is the clear implication that the act of birth brings no innate sin with it. The child is born clear of taint; it is the experience of the growing youth which first brings sin and blots out all consciousness of Paradise. And yet that very Paradise is close to man, and available to him. But it takes the experience of pain and bitter sorrow, even of a loved one's death, to bring us to a realization of Paradise again:

> Thus hast thou plac'd in mans outside

Death to the Common Eye,
That heaven within him might abide,
And close eternitie;
Hence, youth, and folly (mans first shame,)
Are put unto the slaughter,
And serious thoughts begin to tame
The wise-mans-madnes *Laughter*;

(p. 417, ll.29–36)

The end of the poem is a perfect example of Vaughan's ability to express deep, even passionate personal emotion by using Biblical thought and imagery. The prayer to Christ with which he closes the elegy is based clearly enough on part of the fourth verse of the thirty-ninth psalm, 'Lord make me to know my end, and the measure of my days, what it is; that I may know how frail I am.'

O let me (like him,) know my End!
And be as glad to find it,
And whatsoe'r thou shalt Commend,
Still let thy Servant mind it!
Then make my soule white as his owne,
My faith as pure, and steddy,
And deck me, Lord, with the same Crowne
Thou hast crownd him already!

(p. 418, ll.57–64)

These lines imply the full righteousness of the one who had died, William his brother, and is now united with Christ. They plainly echo the famous speech by Balaam, during the Israelites' wanderings, in which he asks to be identified with the righteousness of Jacob:

Who can count the dust of Jacob, and the number of the fourth part of Israel? Let me die the death of the righteous, and let my last end be like his.

(A.V., *Numbers*, Ch. 23, v.10)

In the last two lines, however, Vaughan's use of 'Crowne' has a clear echo of *Revelation*, a book which he uses more than any other book in the Bible and appears to know with an extraordinary intimacy. William has been faithful unto death, and has now been rewarded by receiving the Crown of life; Vaughan pleads for the same end. This is exactly the sense in which the writer of *Revelation* uses it in the second chapter of the book:

> Fear none of these things which thou shalt suffer; behold, the devil shall cast some of you into prison, that ye may be tried; and ye shall have tribulation ten days; be thou faithful unto death, and I will give thee the crown of life.
>
> (A.V., *Revelation*, Ch. 2, v.10)

Even the plea that God shall make his soul as white as the one he laments is taken directly from *Revelation.* No book in the Bible emphasises whiteness as holiness as much as *Revelation*, and Vaughan's earlier reference to the Cross, from which salvation comes, prepares directly for the holiness which he fervently hopes that God has prepared for him, as He did for those 'which came out of great tribulation, and have washed their robes, and made them white in the blood of the Lamb' (A.V., *Revelation*, Ch. 7, v.14).

Already in 'Isaac's Marriage' the 'white days' have been associated directly with the innocence of childhood. Now the soul made white again by the sacrifice of Christ has returned to its original purity. William, if indeed he is the subject of the elegy, as appears most likely, has now passed into the white radiance of Eternity, from which the child originally came.

In this elegy, therefore, Vaughan has placed his view of Innocence within the great drama of the soul restored to God through the sacrifice of Jesus, and he has used some of the most dramatic images of the Old Testament and the New to increase the intensity of his personal lament and plea to Christ himself. It is a lyric of rare beauty and power.

'The Retreate' is entirely concerned with the innocence of 'early days'. There is, in fact, very little in this poem which he has not already introduced in poems placed earlier in the collection. But it is of great interest because it shows how far, and with what confidence, Vaughan has developed his original statement. In 'Isaac's Marriage' the theme was important but it is not the only theme. In other poems, as we have seen, he uses the theme in the context of a wider exploration of the spiritual world. But here in 'The Retreate' there is a total commitment to his idea, and a directness that no earlier poem has possessed. It is announced unashamedly in the opening lines:

> Happy those early dayes! when I
> Shin'd in my Angell-infancy.
>
> (p. 419, ll.1–2)

and is pursued relentlessly to the end:

> And when this dust falls to the urn
> In that state I came return.
>
> (p. 420, ll.31–32)

This is the first time in *Silex Scintillans* that he has pleaded for a complete return to the innocence which he believes he had during his first 'race'.

The first impressive feature of the poem is that Vaughan has sharpened the distinction which he has already implied in earlier poems, between the instinctive or intuitive life of the young soul and the world of rational understanding and intellect which he had learned as innocence receded.

> Before I understood this place
> Appointed for my second race,
> Or taught my soul to fancy ought
> But a white, Celestiall thought,
>
> (p. 419, ll.3–6)

It is most interesting that these two characteristics of the infant life, lack of understanding of the world, and holiness, are not justified by any Biblical reference whatever. Not until the second part of the poem does he draw directly on Biblical sources. They are direct claims, items of personal witness. Vaughan does acknowledge that he was not in Paradise fully, but near enough to the holiness of paradise still, to be constantly aware of it:

> When yet I had not walkt above
> A mile, or two, from my first love,
> And looking back (at that short space,)
> Could see a glimpse of his bright-face;
>
> (p. 419, ll.7–10)

This gives us the second great characteristic of his statement in the poem. Though it is far less dependent upon direct

Biblical context than the three major poems on this theme which have preceded it, it is still a specifically Christian vision. Christ Himself is at the heart of the Paradise he remembers, and the brightness of His face is the essential ingredient of that experience.

Nor is nature treated as beautiful in itself. It is worth noting that there is only one direct mention of nature in the poem and that is even more generalized than in most of Vaughan's poems. Rather is Nature seen in a Platonic role, a manifestation of (two) particular forms of the Eternal Beauty, a reminder of the Glory which does not change. And the 'fleshly dresse' of his mortal life is also Platonic in its implication that the here and now is only the appearance and not the reality. It is also something he wears, like a garment, which is a constant remembrance of the finished dress that once he had:

> When on some *gilded Cloud*, or *flowre*
> My gazing soul would dwell an houre,
> And in those weaker glories spy
> Some shadows of eternity;
> Before I taught my tongue to wound
> My Conscience with a sinfull sound,
> Or had the black art to dispence
> A sev'rall sinne to ev'ry sence,
> But felt through all this fleshly dresse
> Bright *shootes* of everlastingnesse.
>
> (p. 419, ll.11–20)

He has spoken disparagingly of conscience in 'Mans fall, and Recovery', regarding it only as a 'sullen beam'. It is interesting that in 'The Retreate' he blames only himself, seeing conscience as a sort of register which records the sins of the life he has lived as he moves further and further from the Innocence of early childhood. And the picture of this sinful life is much blacker, though brief, than it was in either 'Mans fall, and Recovery' or 'Thou that know'st for whom I mourne'. Every sense is contaminated by the sin he commits and his imagery gives a powerful impression of an entire web of evil and corruption.

The plea for a return to the 'ancient track' which then follows is one Vaughan makes often in *Silex Scintillans*, and is, as we have already seen, a part of his desire to be rid of the new Puritan order which he believes has usurped all the old Church values and traditions. But here it introduces the most specific concept of the original glory of Paradise, which the soul of the new-born child still feels and responds to:

> O how I long to travell back
> And tread again that ancient track!
> That I might once more reach that plaine,
> Where first I left my glorious traine,
> From whence th'Inlightened spirit sees
> That shady City of Palme trees;
>
> (p. 419, ll.21–26)

Here there is a deliberate mingling of Biblical influences. The 'plaine' conveys not only the sense of richness of the earth and settled living which occurs in so many of God's promises in the Old Testament, but also the disappearance of all discord and strife as in the prophecy of Isaiah – 'And the crooked shall be made straight and the rough places plain' (A.V., *Isaiah*, Ch. 40, v.4). And only from this place is the soul, approaching bliss, able to see the Heavenly City.

The symbolism of 'Palme-trees' is exactly right for Vaughan's purpose. It gives us first the vision of righteous souls gathered into God's city, as in the *Book of Psalms*:

> The righteous shall flourish like the palm tree;
> he shall grow like a cedar in Lebanon.
>
> (A.V., *Psalms*, Ch. 92, v.12)

This is the principal interpretation of the palm in Biblical tradition and scholarship and this verse from the *Psalms* is the embodiment of it. But there is also of course the Christian lore associated with the palm as a symbol of greeting and welcome, as in Christ's progress. This is taken up and developed into the symbolism of ultimate victory in the famous passage of the *Book of Revelation* which Vaughan has already used indirectly in 'Thou that know'st for whom I mourne'.

> After this I beheld, and lo, a great multitude, which no man could number, of all nations and kindreds, and people and tongues, stood before the throne, and before the Lamb, clothed with white robes and palms in their hands;

And cried with a loud voice, saying: Salvation to our God which sitteth upon the throne, and unto the Lamb.

(A.V., *Revelation*, Ch. 7, vv.9–10)

From the clarity and brilliance of this vision we are hurled back into sin and debauch. The longer the soul stays on earth the more it is contaminated and loses all purpose. Vaughan's contrast between Heaven and his earthly existence is stark:

But (ah!) my soul with too much stay
Is drunk, and staggers in the way.
Some men a forward motion love,
But I by backward steps would move,
And when this dust falls to the urn
In that state I came return.

(p. 420, ll.27–32)

He chooses to close with an absolutely clear statement of the value and status of his spiritual life. It goes beyond anything we have yet had in *Silex Scintillans*. It is far more than a fond remembrance of the supposed innocence of early childhood. It contains no acknowledgement of the necessity to experience temptation, and commit sin so that we may know the power of salvation, which he expressed in 'Thou that know'st for whom I mourne'. It calls for a quick release from the burdens of his earthly experience and a return to the original joys of the new-born soul.

'The Retreate' is certainly the most direct and single-minded statement of the innocence of childhood in his poetry, and it is easy to see why so many critics and students have interpreted Vaughan as a man who aims for and usually achieves withdrawal from the world and its tumults. But it is, of course, only one lyric and, for all its beauty, gives an over-simplified impression of the poet as a whole. It certainly represents one important strand in his complex personality, but even within his vision of childhood there are many other strands. 'The Retreate', however fine a poem, must be seen within the total context of his religious work.

In 'Joy of my life', the fifth of the poems marked with a plain paragraph mark in *Silex Scintillans*, Vaughan returns briefly to the theme of an original joy and glory which the world has spoiled. There seems little reason to doubt that the poem, like the others in the series, is an elegy for a close relative or friend. It may well be a further Elegy for William.[1]

There are two interesting features of this lyric. First is Vaughan's insistence that the experience of living in the world is full of barriers and obstacles and contrasts with the pure radiance of life before this experience:

> Gods Saints are shining lights: who stays
> Here long must passe
> O're dark hills, swift streames, and steep ways
> As smooth as glasse:
>
> (p. 423, ll.17–20)

Though his picture is not as dark as in 'The Retreate' the statement is very similar. To remain in the world is to become enmeshed with problems and difficulties.

But the second feature, and chief beauty of the poem is his lengthy development of the imagery of stars as chief reminder of the world from which we came. The final stanza is especially interesting:

> They are (indeed,) our Pillar-fires
> Seen as we go,
> They are that Cities shining spires
> We travell too;
> A swordlike gleame
> Kept man for sin
> First *Out*; This beame
> Will guide him *In*.
>
> (p. 423, ll.25–32)

Though man has left the innocence of his first state he is constantly reminded of its glory in the stars, the pillars of Heaven. Vaughan deliberately uses one of the most important Biblical symbols, the pillar. In *Exodus* there is the 'pillar of fire by night' (A.V., Ch. 13, v.21). In *Genesis*, there is the stone which Jacob designates as a pillar, a monument to the mercy and abiding presence of God (A.V., Ch. 28, v.18). To this symbol he adds the Biblical symbolism of the stars, the 'stars of God' as used in the prophecy of *Isaiah* (A.V., Ch. 14, v.13). There are also the eternal beacons of light, as in

[1] For discussion of William's death and its possible effects on Vaughan's life, see Hutchinson, pp. 104–106.

the *Psalms*: 'Praise ye him, sun and moon: praise him all ye stars of light.' (A.V., Ch. 148, v.3).

The contrast between the flashing of the stars and the flashing of the murderer's knife, which ensured the inevitability of sin, gives the poem a most dramatic ending. It is also an illustration of the development of Vaughan's imagery and thought on the innocence of Childhood. If sin is constant, so is the awareness of the glory from which we came. If we came from a world of light, the stars are now sure beacons of light to guide us, and eventually restore us to that same world.

'Corruption' is not directly concerned with the innocence of childhood, but it is worth noting because it considerably develops Vaughan's view of what he terms the 'early days' of man, and thus parallels his vision of the young child and the special status of early childhood:

> Sure, It was so. Man in those early days
>   Was not all stone, and Earth,
> He shin'd a little, and with those weak Rays
>   Had some glimpse of his birth.
> He saw Heaven o'r his head, and knew from whence
>   He came (condemned,) hither,
> And, as first Love draws strongest, so from hence
>   His mind sure progress'd thither.
>
> (p. 440, ll.1–8)

The picture he gives is similar to the one already described, of the young child looking back and remembering the glory he has known. But the difference is that man knows he is operating under the curse. The young child, however, is ignorant of why he has been born into this world. 'The Retreate' began with the assertion of a life full of joy, and the infant 'shin'd'. But early man, already aware of the condemnation, shines only 'a little'. He can remember the home he came from, but already he feels at odds with his natural environment. This passage is particularly important:

> Things here were strange unto him: Swet, and till
>   All was a thorn, or weed,
> Nor did those last, but (like himself,) dyed still
>   As soon as they did *Seed*,
> They seem'd to quarrel with him;
>
> (p. 440, ll.9–13)

By contrast, the one consistent feature of the life of the young child is its unawareness of sin. It is not tainted by the realization of the Fall. But this poem makes us aware, as his 'childhood' poems do not, of the shame of the soul as it looks back and remembers the 'bright days' of Eden.

Despite the great difference between the experience of early man and that of the young child, the poem contains what is arguably his most vivid and detailed picture of the original glory. In earlier poems, as we have seen, he has given us only glimpses. Even in 'The Retreate' his description of it, though confident enough, was very brief. But in this poem he sees it clearly:

> He sigh'd for *Eden*, and would often say
> *Ah! what bright days were those?*
> Nor was Heav'n cold unto him; for each day
> The vally, or the Mountain
> Afforded visits, and still *Paradise* lay
> In some green shade, or fountain.
> Angels lay *Leiger* here; Each Bush, and Cel,
> Each Oke, and high-way knew them,
> Walk but the fields, or sit down at some *wel*,
> And he was sure to view them.
>
> (p. 440, ll.19–28)

Once again, he has used the pastoral imagery of *Genesis* in his description but he has not referred to any specific character or incident. The picture of Paradise contrasts with that of the Heavenly City in 'The Retreate'. The plain and the palm trees have given way now to a landscape of hills, valleys, fountains and the familiar 'green shade' which Vaughan uses so often to designate the tranquillity and beauty of spiritual bliss. Though he hardly ever gives a particular reference to the natural scenery of Breconshire in his poetry, the description here does seem to have the general suggestion of the Usk valley, with its hills, beautifully formed valleys and waterfalls.[1]

The final passage of the poem is of the greatest interest because it shows clearly that for Vaughan the fall of man

[1] The lake of which he writes in 'The Showre' would appear to be Llangorse Lake but it is certainly never identified by name, and is the only reference to a particular place in his religious poems of which one can be reasonably sure.

and loss of innocence in Eden can only be countered by the sudden and complete revelation of the power and glory of God:

> I see, thy Curtains are Close-drawn; Thy bow
>   Looks dim too in the Cloud,
> Sin triumphs still, and man is sunk below
>   The Center, and his shrowd;
> All's in deep sleep, and night; Thick darknes lyes
>   And hatcheth o'r thy people;
> But hark! what trumpets that? what Angel cries
>   *Arise! Thrust in thy sickle.*
>
> (p. 440, ll.33–40)

It has already been made clear in the discussion of the political influences on his poetry that Vaughan sees such a condition of sin and depravity existing in the Britain, and in the Breconshire of his time, that no half measures, no general palliatives would improve it. His vision here is similar. In fact lines thirty-seven and thirty-eight with their grim reminder of 'thick darknes' which 'hatcheth o'r thy people' may well be another allusion to the Puritan regime and not just a general description of the people's sin. Whatever the particular distress that drove him to write it there is no doubting his response.

For his final powerful challenge to the people and the age he returns to the *Book of Revelation*. The passage he has taken as a basis for the lines is from the fourteenth chapter, and the entire chapter has a vital bearing on Vaughan's work. The chapter gives us contrasting pictures; first, the redeemed who sing before the throne of the Lamb, and second, the corrupt of the earth who are symbolized by the people of Babylon. The climax of the chapter is the Fall of Babylon, the entire exposure of corruption upon which it has rested, and finally the Harvest of the World by the Angels:

> And I looked, and beheld a white cloud, and upon the cloud one sat like unto the Son of man, having on his head a golden crown, and in his hand a sharp sickle.
>
> And another angel came out of the temple, crying with a loud voice to him that sat on the cloud, Thrust in thy sickle and reap: for the time is come for thee to reap: for the harvest of the earth is ripe.
>
> (A.V., *Revelation*, Ch. 14, vv.14–15)

Once again Vaughan has used the dramatic imagery of the *Book of Revelation* to sum up his entire vision of the innocence of man's early days, and the joys of Paradise remembered, corrupted by the sin and folly of the world. And there is in this extraordinarily powerful lyric at least the suggestion that some of the sins of man are beyond redemption. If one accepts the full implication of this passage of *Revelation* in his conclusion, there may be no salvation now, only destruction for the wickedness that has been committed. In this Vaughan's attitude seems to be very similar to that expressed in his second 'Day of Judgement' poem (p. 530).

'The Burial Of an Infant' returns to the theme of childhood itself. There is no picture of Paradise in the poem, but there is, instead, a complete concentration on the life and death of a very young infant. Though the poem is only twelve lines long, it gives a remarkably clear and detailed picture of the period shortly after birth, and is the only one of Vaughan's poems to be entirely devoted to this experience. It may fittingly be used as a summary of his view of early childhood in the first part of *Silex Scintillans*.

The first stanza gives us a parallel between the life of the infant and the blossom, and is expressed with great feeling and tenderness:

> Blest Infant Bud, whose Blossome-life
> Did only look about, and fal,
> Wearyed out in a harmles strife
> Of tears, and milk, the food of all;
>
> (p. 450, ll.1–4)

The play on the word 'fal', conveying the falling of the blossom and also the falling about of the young child, reveals great delicacy and the implication that the young child has all the naturalness and beauty of the blossom in nature is clear. In the third and fourth lines the innocence of the child is developed into a statement which includes all children. The softness of touch is sustained in the poignant coupling of 'tears, and milk'.

In the second stanza Vaughan underscores the theme of child innocence in a way which makes it absolutely plain that for him no theological dogma can prove the guilt of the infant soul:

> Sweetly didst thou expire: Thy soul
> Flew home unstain'd by his new kin,
> For ere thou knew'st how to be foul,
> Death *wean'd* thee from the world, and sin.
>
> (p. 450, ll.5–8)

When one reflects upon the ideas which prevailed in his own Church at the time he was writing, to which reference has already been made, his statement is both brave and challenging. It also shows great skill. Vaughan replaces the image of the blossom by that of the bird and implies that the soul of the child soars into the freedom of Paradise, returning to the joy it has known so recently. And the image of death in the fourth line is very striking. Instead of the mother weaning the child to prepare it for the world, death weans the child from the sins of that world in order to prepare it for Eternity with God.

The third and final stanza shows the same tenderness, and respect for the innocence of the infant. This is an elegy for the sweetness and softness of one whom the world has not touched:

> Softly rest all thy Virgin-Crums!
> *Lapt* in the sweets of thy young breath,
> Expecting till thy Saviour Comes
> To *dresse* them, and *unswadle* death.
>
> (p. 450, ll.9–12)

There is surely play upon 'Virgin' here. The young child is fresh and unspoiled but that child also bears similarity to the infant Jesus, born of the Virgin. 'Lapt' conveys the sense of water gently caressing the child. But the contrast is swift and dramatic. The child has committed no sin and may therefore rest in the confident expectation that Christ will give him the dress of righteousness. Vaughan's use of 'unswadle' is one of the most powerful conceits in all his poetry and is a superb summary of his thought and feeling in the lyric. The earthly mother will no longer dress the child, but Christ will dress him and by so doing will take away all the trappings of death so that its power is gone. The association of the earthly child with the Christ-child, begun in the first line of the stanza, is completed now by the use of a word normally associated with the birth of Christ – the swaddling clothes. Moreover birth and death are brought together in this last line. This death is birth into newness of life.

'The Burial Of an Infant' is certainly the shortest lyric he composed upon this subject but Vaughan never surpassed it as an exposition of the close association between infancy and the mystery of eternal life. For all its compactness and depth, 'The Retreate' does not have the sensitivity nor the homeliness of this lyric. There is no direct Biblical quotation in the poem, but its entire thought would seem to spring easily and naturally from the homeliness of the Bible narrative of Jesus himself, when he set a child in the midst of his disciples and hearers and warned them that unless they became as little children they would not enter into the Kingdom of Heaven. In this sense 'The Burial Of an Infant' is a well nigh perfect exposition of his theme. It is also one of the most concise lyrics he ever wrote, and easily one of the most moving.

'The Burial Of an Infant' is the last poem in the first part of *Silex Scintillans* in which Vaughan treats early childhood as a major theme. In the second part of his work there are in fact only two poems, 'The Seed growing secretly' and 'Childe-hood' which give any substantial statement of infancy as a state apart. There are several important poems in which the humility of the child is considered as a vital preparation for entrance into the Kingdom of God, but these will be considered later.

'The Seed growing secretly' is one of the most complex and intense of all Vaughan's poems, and its imagery and thought deserve considerable study within the Biblical framework Vaughan has used. The subject of childhood is treated directly only in the early part of the poem but the infinite value of that early experience is implied right through the lyric as Vaughan surveys all the reaches of the hidden spiritual growth.

The text which he cites, but does not quote, at the beginning of the poem is from *St. Mark's gospel*:

And he said, So is the Kingdom of God, as if a man should cast seed into the ground ...

(A.V., *Mark*, Ch. 4, v.26)

The first stanza is built directly upon the contrast between the pleasures and pursuits of the worldly man with his eyes upon the riches and power of this world, and the simplicity of the poor man, who by clear implication has his eyes upon a spiritual goal:

If this worlds friends might see but once
What some poor man may often feel,
Glory, and gold, and Crowns and Thrones
They would soon quit and learn to kneel.

(p. 510, ll.1–4)

Vaughan uses no specific Biblical reference here, but he is drawing on a truth which is both stated directly and implied in the Old and New Testaments. The assertion in *Isaiah* will serve as the basic truth, which is rendered in various forms throughout the Bible:

But to this man will I look, even to him that is poor and of a contrite spirit, and trembleth at my word:

(A.V., *Isaiah*, Ch. 66, v.2)

Vaughan therefore begins his exploration with a vision of spiritual riches. But the principal creative tension of the poem springs from his realization that he has lost this glory which some men can still feel instinctively, and which he had once in great measure:

My dew, my dew! my early love,
My souls bright food, thy absence kills!
Hover not long, eternal Dove!
Life without thee is loose and spills.

(p. 510, ll.5–8)

'Dew', which Vaughan uses very frequently in his religious verse is one of his main symbols of spiritual refreshment. In this he is following closely a multitude of stories and statements in the Old and New Testaments. Isaiah, for example, speaks of 'the dew of God' bringing the people to life again after the state of death, which was the captivity of Babylon:

> Thy dead men shall live, together with my dead body shall they arise. Awake and sing, ye that dwell in dust: for thy dew is as the dew of herbs, and the earth shall cast out the dead.
>
> (A.V., *Isaiah*, Ch. 26, v.19)

Whether that verse was in his mind or not, it is exactly in this sense that Vaughan also is using it as the visitation of God which breaks the captivity of sin and brings the soul back to life. And Vaughan deepens the symbolism by his image of the Dove, the pure one, symbolizing the innocence and simplicity of the new-born child, as at the Baptism of Jesus, when the Holy Spirit appeared in the form of a dove. This is a careful preparation for the account of his own childhood:

> Something I had, which long ago
> Did learn to suck, and sip, and taste,
> But now grown sickly, sad and slow,
> Doth fret and wrangle, pine and waste.
>
> (p. 511, ll.9–12)

This is the development of his concept of the child's nearness to God in early infancy, which he has explored throughout the first part of his work. The picture here is of the infant who finds it completely natural to receive the love of God. He is completely open to it, so that he takes the spiritual refreshment of God, brought by the Dove, as easily and spontaneously as he sucks his mother's milk. But as he grows he moves away from God, he can take it no longer and grows into sickness, not health. The prayer which follows is a desperate plea for the presence of God. Once again, as in many of the poems in the first part of his work, the implication is that he needs the spiritual nourishment he knew as a child, if he is to maintain his spiritual life:

> O spred thy sacred wings and shake
> One living drop! one drop life keeps!
> If pious griefs Heavens joys awake,
> O fill his bottle! thy childe weeps!
>
> (p. 511, ll.13–16)

In the first line of the stanza he develops his image of the Holy Dove and once more uses a well known Biblical phrase of the Authorized Version. This phrase is most used in prophecy, especially in the prophetic judgement of *Jeremiah*:

> For thus saith the Lord: Behold he shall fly as an eagle, and shall spread his wings over Moab.
>
> (A.V., *Jeremiah*, Ch. 48, v.40)

But Vaughan's plea is for deliverance, not destruction. In the last line of the stanza he intensifies his cry by quoting directly from *Psalms*, a phrase which he has used in the prayer in 'The Mount of Olives', in which he alludes also to the death of his 'dearest and nearest relatives' (p. 167, l.5). The psalm is indeed an anguished cry to God for deliverance from the oppression of his enemies:

> Thou tellest my wanderings: put thou my tears into thy bottle: are they not in thy book?
>
> (A.V., *Psalms*, Ch. 56, vv.8–9)

However, Vaughan cleverly inverts this, and asks for the dew of God in the bottle of his life, so that his tears may cease. It is a good example of the way in which he very often plays upon the imagery of the Authorized Version.

From the song of mourning which covers the first five stanzas he changes now to a celebration of the fruits of that secret life of which Christ spoke. In this celebration he appears to take his personal visionary stimulus from the prophetic books of the Old Testament and the *Book of Revelation* in the New.

> For thy eternal, living wells
> None stain'd or wither'd shall come near:
> A fresh, immortal *green* there dwells,
> And spotless *white* is all the wear.
>
> (p. 511, ll.21–24)

His 'eternal, living wells' is firmly based on Bible images, whether one reads it in *Isaiah*:

> Therefore with joy shall ye draw water out of the wells of salvation.
>
> (A.V., *Isaiah*, Ch. 12, v.3)

or the familiar gospel story of Jesus and the Woman of Samaria, with Christ's promise that 'the water that I shall give him shall be to him a well of water springing up into everlasting life' (A.V., *John*, Ch. 4, v.14). It is, of course, one of Vaughan's favourite symbols, in which he usually follows closely Biblical symbolism. 'Religion', as we have seen, depends very largely upon it in its closing stanzas.

In the last two lines of the stanza Vaughan gives a picture of Heaven, signified by the two colours, green and white. Hutchinson explains this by pointing out that 'green is the colour most universally noticeable in natural scenery,' while white means in Welsh 'fair', 'happy', 'holy' and 'blessed'.[1]

There is no doubt that green suggests the natural scene; no doubt either that Vaughan's use of 'white' may sometimes have been prompted by its identification in his mind with holiness. But in this particular stanza, which Hutchinson quotes, there is surely a much stronger reason for his choice of these two colours. His picture of Eternity is clearly influenced by Biblical images and symbols. 'Green' is associated with the abundance of the earth and the sheer nourishment of life at the very beginning of the *Book of Genesis*. The writer there puts into God's mouth the confident assertion:

> And to every beast of the earth, and to every fowl of the air, and to everything that creepeth upon the earth, wherein there is life, I have given every green herb for meat: and it was so.
>
> (A.V., *Genesis*, Ch. 1, v.30)

And its sacredness is marked in one of the principal visions of the *Book of Revelation*:

> And it was commanded them that they should not hurt the green of the earth, nor any green thing,neither any tree; but only those men which have not the seal of God in their foreheads.
>
> (A.V., *Revelation*, Ch. 9, v.4)

Further, the huge importance of 'white' in the visions revealed in the *Book of Revelation* has already been noted. *Revelation*, in fact, would seem to be the principal source of Vaughan's picture here.

This picture of Eternity is not, in any case, isolated in the poem. It is part of a much larger vision which takes much of its dramatic colour and scope quite directly from *Revelation*.

[1] Hutchinson, op. cit., pp. 162–163.

After a stanza in which he elaborates upon 'greenness' as the sustenance of the soul, feeding it in secret and observed only by God, he celebrates God's glory in a stanza of sheer praise:

> If those bright joys he singly sheds,
> On thee, were all met in one Crown,
> Both Sun and Stars would hide their heads;
> And Moons, though full, would get them down.
>
> (p. 511, ll.29–32)

It is above all the 'Crown' which supplies the key to the passage. Sun, moon and stars are often linked in Biblical imagery, in *Genesis*, the *Psalms*, and the prophets, notably *Isaiah*. But it is only in *Revelation* that we have the great vision of all these natural lights, being made subject to a greater glory:

> And there appeared a great wonder in heaven; a woman clothed with the sun, and the moon under her feet, and upon her head a crown of twelve stars.
>
> (A.V., *Revelation*, Ch. 12, v.1)

Vaughan has employed all the same four images in his vision of the natural world kneeling in submission to God, their maker. It would be straining credulity to argue that his combination of them is sheer coincidence, especially in a poem so influenced by the vision of *Revelation*.

The last four stanzas of the poem return to the theme of the secret life which is hidden with God and to the contrast which Vaughan drew in the first stanza, between the quest for public power and glory and the deep, sure riches of an inner life, lived in quietness. There are two most striking features. The first is his reference to 'Conscience'. In several poems in the first part of his work, he has called attention to the primacy of conscience, the only guide to truth now that the sure instincts of the early life have left him. Here he still speaks of Conscience with great reverence:

> What needs a Conscience calm and bright
> Within it self an outward test?
> Who breaks his glass to take more light,
> Makes way for storms into his rest.
>
> (p. 511, ll.41–44)

Vaughan takes the Biblical interpretation of Conscience without any major qualifications. In all his poetry is the testimony and secret judgement of the soul, which either gives its approval to actions that it thinks good, or reproaches itself with those which it believes to be evil. That capacity of the soul to evaluate and judge is, of course, frequently stressed in the various epistles towards the end of the New Testament. Vaughan's emphasis here, as one would expect in this summing up of his long statement upon the value of the inner life, is that the operation of just and proper conscience is secret, and therefore its judgements come from the inner soul. He is so concerned to reject, with some scorn, the argument that the believer should subject himself to some external test, that one wonders whether this is yet another reference to the Puritan fondness for public testimony of faith, which Vaughan so much detests. Whether he had any specific target in mind or not, it is certain that he sees conscience as the 'calm' and quiet instrument of the soul.

The second outstanding feature is that Vaughan has chosen to end his poem with another direct reference to one of the visions of the *Book of Revelation*. His 'white winged reapers' are central characters in the great prophetic vision of the fourteenth chapter of *Revelation*, which he has already used in his poem, 'Corruption'.

> Then bless thy secret growth, nor catch
> At noise, but thrive unseen and dumb;
> Keep clean, bear fruit, earn life and watch
> Till the white winged Reapers come!
>
> (p. 511, ll.45–48)

This must be one of the most searching and confident conclusions he ever wrote. It is a clear and concise summary of his essential message and places the entire quality of the secret spiritual life within the context of a full preparation here and now for the coming of Eternity, which will restore us to the joys which once we have known. It is an ending which has great dramatic power and intensity, and it has all the surprise and joy of direct revelation.

'Childe-hood' is the only other poem in the second part of *Silex Scintillans* which treats the theme of child innocence directly and therefore is his final statement on the world of the child as a state apart, if, in fact, the ordering of his poems in the collection is considered as a deliberate progression, not merely a chance arrangement.

It is a quite substantial statement embracing the entire poem, and one in which Christ's warning 'Except ye become as little children ...' would seem to be implicit from first to last.

> I cannot reach it; and my striving eye
> Dazles at it, as at eternity.
> Were now that Chronicle alive,
> Those white designs which children drive,
> And the thoughts of each harmless hour,
> With their content too in my pow'r,
> Quickly would I make my path even,
> And by meer playing go to Heaven.
>
> (p. 520, ll.1–8)

It is important that one takes special note of the poem's opening contrast between the world of holiness which the young child knows and responds to instinctively and the impossibility of reaching it again. Now it is Eternity, a far off vision of glory, but then it was natural and the child could bring it within his grasp even by the most natural instinct, that of play. His statement of child innocence does not add to what we have had in the first part of *Silex Scintillans*, but his acknowledgement that he is merely dazzled by the brilliance of it and can never get there, is sharper and reveals a greater frustration than earlier.

The second main characteristic of this lyric is the very uncompromising view he takes of all affairs of the adult world. He has never regarded the adult life as at all free from the possibility of sin but his attitude does now seem to have hardened very considerably.

> Why should men love
> A Wolf, more than a Lamb or Dove?
> Or choose hell-fire and brimstone steams
> Before bright stars, and Gods own beams?
>
> (p. 521, ll.9–12)

His vision of the world here is very similar indeed to the

one contained in the gospel of John where 'men loved darkness rather than light, because their deeds were evil' (A.V., *John*, Ch. 3, v.19). But Vaughan has not usually shown sin as such a conscious, deliberate act; it is more often blind folly but here his judgement is that grown-up people usually choose hell.

At this stage of his writing during which he composed the blood-guilt poems, which we have already discussed, he was filled with black despair, at the sheer accumulation of murder and destruction, and put it down to man's positive preference for evil. Whether or not the war years and their aftermath had created the particular depression one senses here, it is certain that he sees the memory of childhood as the one safe place, the refuge from the dirt and corruption of life as he is experiencing it:

> Since all that age doth teach, is ill,
> Why should I not love childe-hood still?
> Why if I see a rock or shelf,
> Shall I from thence cast down my self,
> Or by complying with the world,
> From the same precipice be hurl'd?
> Those observations are but foul
> Which make me wise to lose my soul.
>
> (p. 521, ll.19–26)

The 'rock' is a powerful symbol here, containing as it would for Vaughan the Biblical association of 'the rock which is higher than I' (A.V., *Psalms*, Ch. 61, v.2). When linked with 'cast down' it has also the very strong suggestion of the second temptation as recorded by Matthew, in which Christ is asked by the Devil to throw himself down in order to prove His power. Vaughan's assertion that by allowing himself to be thrown into the world he will lose his own soul, re-enforces the impression that he is deeply aware of the temptations of Christ. Those who listen to this beguiling voice will simply cast themselves away, with all the frightful consequences.

Is there any evidence that he softens his attitude to man's sin as he develops his theme? It would seem that far from softening, his condemnation is even sharper than in the opening:

Dear, harmless age! the short, swift span,
Where weeping virtue parts with man;
Where love without lust dwells, and bends
What way we please, without self-ends.

(p. 521, ll.31–34)

The clear contrast here is savage. Childhood is not only without taint, but is complete with virtue and love. The adult world is without innocence or virtue. It is self-centred and embodies lust instead of love.

Vaughan's final statement in the poem is an acknowledgement that the entire world of early childhood is one of 'mysteries'. It is the only occasion in all his poetry of childhood that he seems to admit it is indescribable. But the whole tone of the passage which closes this lyric encourages us to accept the mystery as an essential part of that truth which we cannot here know:

An age of mysteries! which he
Must live twice, that would Gods face see;
Which *Angels* guard, and with it play,
Angels! which foul men drive away.

How do I study now, and scan
Thee, more than ere I studyed man,
And onely see through a long night
Thy edges, and thy bordering light!
O for thy Center and mid-day!
For sure that is the *narrow* way.

(p. 521, ll.35–44)

There are three important points in this statement. The first is his reference to the necessity of living 'twice', by which it is probable that he means a spiritual re-birth, sometimes termed second birth. Second the fact that he does not count himself among those who can see 'Gods face'. He is on the fringes of the experience but his phrase 'long night' shows clearly that he is a long way from that vision he yearns for. Finally, although there is much less Biblical allusion in his poem than in some of the others on this theme, the world of the child, whether it follows first or second birth, takes on very much the quality of revelation. It is a world in which angels are a part of the natural order of things. The picture is very similar to that in 'Corruption', in which 'Angels lay Leiger'.

Vaughan's last complete statement of the innocence of childhood is thus partly a re-capitulation of earlier statements, and partly a new experience. The difference is that now he sees the subject far more within the context of man's sin and shame, and his picture of man is much sharper and more uncompromising than earlier. This gives to his vision of childhood here a greater dramatic urgency. Now it is no longer merely a world of innocence to which he longs to return, but a rock to which he must desperately fly to escape the foulness of the world.

In addition to poems which treat childhood as a state of innocence, apart and free from the corruption of the world, there are in *Silex Scintillans* a number of poems which either imply or directly state a kindred theme in his work. This is the capacity of God's creatures, including the various parts of inanimate nature to respond to the call of the Creator himself. Young infants are sometimes included directly in his statement; sometimes, however, there is merely the general inference that once we were all able to make this instinctive response, and now only the new-born can achieve it. Most of these lyrics occur in the first part of *Silex Scintillans*, and thus re-enforce the impression that he is more directly concerned with childhood and its related interests in the poems written between 1648 and 1650 than in the second section of his work.

Early in the first part of his work, 'The Call', which explores the call of God and the need for repentance in his own life, begins with a direct reference to the capacity for instinctive response to God's love, which he has lost:

Come my heart! come my head
  In sighes, and teares!
'Tis now, since you have laine thus dead
  Some twenty years;

(p. 416, ll.1–4)

Writing in his late twenties Vaughan looks back on his own childhood twenty years earlier, and he speaks quite directly of the entire period after childhood as one of emotional and intellectual death, from which state only God can awake him.

In 'The Morning-watch' he begins his poem with a confident assertion that the spiritual life is all freshness, a spontaneous and instinctive response to the naturalness and harmony of God's creation:

> O Joyes! Infinite sweetness! with what flowres,
> And shoots of glory, my soul breakes, and buds!
>
> (p. 424, ll.1–2)

The entire re-emergence of his spiritual life is given the imagery of the infant life of Nature. Concerned as he is with the passage from spiritual death to the soul's re-birth he uses 'dew' as he did in 'The Seed growing secretly' as the direct visitation of God which is able to break the power of sin:

> All the long houres
> Of night, and Rest
> Through the still shrouds
> Of sleep, and Clouds,
> This Dew fell on my Breast;
> O how it *Blouds*,
> And *Spirits* all my Earth! heark! In what Rings,
> And *Hymning Circulations* the quick world
> Awakes, and sings;
>
> (p. 424, ll.3–11)

In both thought and imagery Vaughan's emphasis throughout the whole poem is on the joy of the instinctive life, and the necessity of reaching once again, by a process of re-birth the freshness and youth which one knew when young.

In 'Chearfulness' the image of the re-birth of his soul is now that of the bird responding immediately to the call of its creator, and kept entirely by the power of God:

> Lord, with what courage, and delight
> I doe each thing
> When thy least breath sustaines my wing!
> I shine, and move
> Like those above;
> And (with much gladnesse
> Quitting sadnesse,)
> Make me faire dayes of every night.
>
> (p. 428, ll.1–8)

Though the image has changed, the main theme of the poem remains, as in 'The Morning-watch', the enormous importance of the immediate and instinctive response of the soul to God. One notes that in none of these poems is any importance placed upon the reason or intellect. Sometimes, in fact, Vaughan suggests that these may be an actual impediment to the work of grace. In 'Distraction' for example, Vaughan declares that the whole process of growth, implying both physical and mental development, actually frustrates the progress of the spirit and causes acute depression:

> Hadst thou
> Made me a starre, a pearle, or a rain-bow,
> The beames I then had shot
> My light had lessend not,
> But now
> I find my selfe the lesse, the more I grow;
> The world
> Is full of voices; Man is call'd, and hurl'd
> By each, he answers all,
> Knows ev'ry note, and call,
> Hence, still
> Fresh dotage tempts, or old usurps his will.
> (p. 413, ll.5–16)

The direct contrast between the three symbols of natural splendour in the Universe, star, pearl and rainbow, and the unnatural misery of man who declines as he grows, is most striking and yet again underlines the truth that by so-called growth man has lost the capacity of instinctive response to his Creator, which he had only when young.

The last stanza of 'The Passion' takes up the same lament. Faced with the enormity of Christ's most agonizing sacrifice he craves the sure instinct to be able to respond:

> O blessed Lamb!
> That took'st my sinne,
> That took'st my shame
> How shall thy dust thy praises sing!
> I would I were
> One hearty tear!

One constant spring!
Then would I bring
Thee two small mites, and be at strife
Which should most vie,
My heart, or eye,
Teaching my years
In smiles, and tears
To weep, to sing, thy *Death*, my *Life*.
(pp. 431–432, ll.43–56)

Once again he selects images which suggest a completely spontaneous movement. It is as useless to command the water of the tear not to flow as it is to try to stop the water of the spring. Only this completely natural and un-forced movement towards God can bring him to the place where he can offer just the poverty of his own soul, all that he has, to Christ his crucified Lord. Vaughan's quick combination of the Lamb that taketh away the sins of the world and the poor widow of the Gospel narrative who 'of her penury hath cast in all the living that she had' (A.V., *Luke*, Ch. 21, v.4), is very characteristic of his style in so many of his religious lyrics.

Two stanzas in the early part of 'Rules *and* Lessons' return to the theme of the joys of infancy and early youth. Here it is the very youth of the world that he celebrates; it is a vision of the innocence and spontaneity of the natural world which God has created:

Walk with thy fellow-creatures: note the *hush*
And *whispers* among them. There's not a *Spring*,
Or *Leafe* but hath his *Morning-hymn*; Each *Bush*
And *Oak* doth know *I AM*; canst thou not sing?
O leave thy Cares, and follies! go this way
And thou art sure to prosper all the day.
(p. 436, ll.13–18)

Once more Vaughan depicts man as impoverished and restless because he has lost the capacity to respond instinctively to the joys of the Creator. Every particular mode of nature rejoices; man alone has no voice. Later he develops the imagery of 'morning' and 'youth' in a passage of great lyrical beauty:

Mornings are *Mysteries*; the first worlds *Youth*,
Mans *Resurrection*, and the futures *Bud*
Shrowd in their births: The Crown of Life, light, truth
Is stil'd their *starre*, the *stone*, and *hidden food*.
Three *blessings* wait upon them, two of which
Should move; They make us *holy, happy*, rich.
(p. 436, ll.25–30)

Vaughan's exploration of Time is important. Whatever Hermetical and other mystical influences there may be upon him he is clearly deeply influenced by the great morning scenes depicted in the Bible, notably the first dawn of Creation and also very possibly the Resurrection morning. Fusing the great historical passages of the Bible as a record of past events, with the climactic passages of the New to produce a vision of the future, he brings the whole of Time to the moment of Revelation – 'The Crown of life'. One notices that the 'first worlds youth' symbolizes the glory of the original creation, unspoiled by sin, whereas man's only experience of complete freshness is in re-birth. The innocence of the child has been irrevocably lost.

In 'Christs Nativity', the political inferences of which have already been discussed, the Birth of Jesus reminds him again of the ready response of all other creatures, except man, to the call of God. In imagery not dissimilar to that he has used in 'Chearfulness' and 'The Passion' he longs for the same quality in his own life, that he may praise God as he should:

I would I were some *Bird*, or Star,
Flutt'ring in woods, or lifted far
Above this *Inne*
And Rode of sin!
Then either Star, or *Bird*, should be
Shining, or singing still to thee.
(p. 442, ll.13–18)

'Admission' is a most intimate confession of his utter dependence on God and there is an image in the third stanza of the poem which summarizes the relationship of the re-born spirit with the God who has forgiven him:

Wee are thy Infants, and suck thee; If thou
But hide, or turn thy face,

Because where thou art, yet, we cannot go,
We send tears to the place,
These find thee out, and though our sins
Drove thee away,
Yet with thy love that absence wins
Us double pay.

(p. 453, ll.17–24)

The identification of God with the parent who loves but has to train his infant is familiar in all religious literature, and was used freely by Donne, and especially by Herbert. But the frank and complete acknowledgement that man reborn has to become again as an infant who 'sucks' the love of God his Father is absolutely characteristic of Vaughan's entire thought and imagery throughout the whole of the first part of *Silex Scintillans.*

There are very few direct images of the value of the spontaneous and instinctive life, recalling the innocence of childhood, in the second part of his work. He is pre-occupied with other themes, and notably the child as a symbol of humility, which will be discussed later. But there are a few poems in which he returns, albeit fleetingly, to his earlier interest.

'Jesus weeping' (first poem) is a short but extremely powerful denunciation of the sin which hurts Christ. Ostensibly the subject of his wrath is the Jews, but there are distinct political undertones here. The murderers of the Puritan period are plainly in his mind. But the contrasting picture he draws is most moving and dramatic:

Dear *Jesus* weep on! pour this latter
Soul-quickning rain, this living water
On their dead hearts; but (O my fears!)
They will drink blood, that despise tears.
My dear, bright Lord! my Morning-star!
Shed this live-dew on fields which far
From hence long for it! shed it there,
Where the starv'd earth groans for one tear!

(pp. 502–503, ll.9–16)

The presentation of Jesus as 'Morning star' follows closely the only direct reference in the Bible, from the closing verses of the Book of Revelation:

I Jesus have sent mine angel to testify unto you these things in the churches. I am the root and the offspring of David, and the bright and morning-star.

(A.V., *Revelation*, Ch. 22, v.16)

The image of the tear which men reject, preferring blood instead, sustains the entire passage, and it is surely no surprise that the tear of Christ becomes first 'soul-quickening rain' and then 'this live-dew', an image he uses so frequently. But the important point is that for Vaughan the tear is not a symbol of shame and sadness but a call to repentance from the depravity and crime of the Civil War period and the sins committed daily in the name of the new Puritan regime. Only the 'dew', the direct visitation of God (in this instance), in the person of Christ, can blot out such sin.

In the first part of 'The Rain-bow' Vaughan returns to the theme of the world when young. It is a passage of dazzling beauty, recalling the original glory of Creation, and though man has sinned and fallen from Grace the rainbow is the symbol now of the eternal truce between man and God:

Still yong and fine! but what is still in view
We slight as old and soil'd, though fresh and new.
How bright wert thou, when *Shems* admiring eye
Thy burnisht, flaming *Arch* did first descry!
When *Terah, Nahor, Haran, Abram, Lot*,
The youthful worlds gray fathers in one knot,
Did with intentive looks watch every hour
For thy new light, and trembled at each shower!

(p. 509, ll.1–8)

This is only one of many passages in his work in which God's promises are depicted as fresh and new. Vaughan is at pains to equate the faithfulness of God with the original glory of the 'youthful world'. Time and again he returns to this theme of the first wonder of Creation and although there is no picture here of the joys of Eden, he manages to recapture some of the young world's glory through which we can discern the majesty of God Himself.

The second part of *Silex Scintillans* is, however, much more concerned with childhood as a symbol of humility, the way by which man re-born can best prepare to serve in the

Kingdom of God. This is the third and final major statement on childhood in Vaughan's work and though there are only a few poems which declare the theme directly they contain substantial statements and must be examined in some detail.

The first is 'Palm-Sunday', a highly personalized and very moving account of Christ's entry into Jerusalem. Vaughan bases the first part of the poem on Luke's narrative. He depicts Jesus as coming, weeping to the city to receive the accolades of the people. It enables him to present a quick and vivid contrast at the outset of his lyric:

> The King of grief, the man of sorrow
> Weeping still, like the wet morrow,
> Your shades and freshness comes to borrow.
> (p. 501, ll.4–6)

The passage about the children is based on a reference in Matthew's gospel and it gives him the opportunity to present Palm-Sunday as a great celebration of the youth of the world:

> Hark! how the children shril and high
> *Hosanna* cry,
> Their joys provoke the distant skie,
> Where thrones and Seraphins reply,
> And their own Angels shine and sing
> In a bright ring:
> Such yong, sweet mirth
> Makes heaven and earth
> Joyn in a joyful Symphony,
> (p. 501, ll.18–26)

It is easy to see why Vaughan, who gives to children such a special status, sees them as the very centre of the joyful scene. Even his reference to angels is interesting, implying, as it appears to do, that the children have angels in heaven to guard them, and that these angels rejoice in Paradise, so that the whole of Creation performs an act of praise. The imagery of youth is then extended to the animal kingdom:

> The harmless, yong and happy Ass,
> Seen long before this came to pass,
> Is in these joys an high partaker
> Ordain'd, and made to bear his Maker.
> (p. 502, ll.27–30)

There are two points of considerable importance here. The first is that Vaughan stresses the role of the children in order to make clear their simplicity and humility. The ass is of course a further symbol of complete humility, and this is only the first of three poems in this second part of *Silex Scintillans* in which the ass is used to illustrate the chief moral point Vaughan is making. The second feature of the poem is that Vaughan sees the ass as a complete fulfilment of Old Testament Prophecy. Christ comes to complete the work of grace which God has purposed from the beginning of time.

In the last two stanzas of the poem, he sees himself as a child again, rejoicing with those other children of whom he has spoken, but the passage takes on once again the style and substance of a special Divine vision:

> Then like the *Palm*, though wrong, I'le bear,
> I will be still a childe, still meek
> As the poor Ass, which the proud jear,
> And onely my dear *Jesus* seek.
>
> If I lose all, and must endure
> The proverb'd griefs of holy *Job*,
> I care not, so I may secure
> But one *green Branch* and a *white robe.*
>
> (p. 502, ll.39–46)

This complete identification of the child and the ass serves to point the need for meekness in face of the trials which beset every Christian. Vaughan's own misery at the deep conflicts and bitterness of his age have already been made clear, and 'Palm-Sunday' must take its place with those other poems, notably 'Abels blood' and 'The Men of War' in which he cries out for the Christian qualities of forgiveness and meekness to replace the desire for revenge. But he does not stop there. Once more it is to the great vision of the *Book of Revelation* that he turns, to be assured that his place in Paradise is secure; as in 'The Seed growing secretly' he places all his emphasis on 'green', the sacred symbol of life, and 'white' the symbol of holiness in *Revelation* (A.V., *Revelation*, Ch. 9, v.4, and Ch. 7, v.14)

'The Men of War', which appears later in this second part of his work, has already been discussed in the context of the strong political pressures which were being exerted upon him, and the inducements which the Puritan authorities were apparently offering him to change his entire stance towards them. But one passage of the poem is especially worthy of note in the context of his consideration of the child as a symbol of true Christian simplicity and humility. It is all the more striking because it occurs immediately after his reference to the 'lure' held out to him:

> Dear *Jesus* give me patience here,
> And faith to see my Crown as near
> And almost reach'd, because 'tis sure
> If I hold fast and slight the *Lure*.
> Give me humility and peace,
> Contented thoughts, innoxious ease,
> A sweet, revengeless, quiet minde,
> And to my greatest haters kinde.
> Give me, my God! a heart as milde
> And plain, as when I was a childe;
>
> (p. 517, ll.37–46)

There is, first, an air of weary resignation in these lines which matches exactly the description Vaughan himself gave of his emotional condition, and perhaps his physical condition also:

> By the last *Poems* in the book (were not that *mistake* here prevented) you would judge all to be *fatherless*, and the *Edition* posthume; for (indeed) *I was nigh unto death*, and am still at no great distance from it; which was the necessary reason for that solemn and accomplished *dress*, you will now finde this *impression* in.
>
> (p. 392, ll.21–26)

Certainly his reference to the Crown as 'near and almost reach'd,' re-enforces the impression that he thought he might die. He would not speak, in any terms known to the Bible and especially the *Book of Revelation*, of his crown being realized in this life.

Secondly he re-asserts his belief that the child knows only meekness and 'plain' dealing. He prays now, and very much in the context of the enmity and bitterness of the Commonwealth period, for all revenge to be taken from his mind. He acknowledges the fact that some men hated him very much; this is presumably a reference not only to the bitter division which the War and its aftermath had caused in the life of the local community, but also to the vehemence with which he had held to the Royalist, and particularly the Anglican cause, in his public actions, his refusal to take any public office despite inducements, and finally many quite open attacks on Puritan doctrine and practice in the poems themselves.

There is considerable development of the theme of the urgent need for Christian humility in the very next poem in his collection, 'The Ass', the second of the three poems in which he uses the ass as a major symbol.

'The Ass' is probably the most fervent and developed plea for a return to the Christ-like qualities of goodness, peace and love in all his work, and its opening lines spell out unashamedly the drama of his own spiritual conflicts:

> Thou! who didst place me in this busie street
> Of flesh and blood, where two ways meet:
> The *One* of goodness, peace and life,
> The *other* of death, sin and strife;
> Where frail visibles rule the minde,
> And present things finde men most kinde:
> Where obscure cares the *mean* defeat,
> And splendid vice destroys the *great*;
> As thou didst set no law for me,
> But that of perfect liberty,
> Which neither tyres, nor doth corrode,
> But is a *Pillow* not a *Load*:
>
> (p. 518, ll.1–12)

If he searches for the God of righteousness, peace and love, who has been blotted out in men's minds during the years of war and dissension, then he must recognize that there is only one law, the law of Christ which has replaced the many rules and laws of the Jews. The Authorized version does, of course, use the adjective 'perfect' of God's liberty.

> But whoso looketh into the perfect law of liberty, and continueth therein, he being not a forgetful hearer, but a doer of the work, this man shall be blessed in his deed.
>
> (A.V., *James*, Ch. 1, v.25)

Vaughan was also, as one knows, very conversant with the eighth chapter of the *Epistle to the Romans* on the nineteenth verse of which he based his 'And do they so?' The twenty-first verse of that same chapter provides the most famous proclamation of the new liberty to be found in the New Testament:

> Because the creature itself also shall be delivered from the bondage of corruption into the glorious liberty of the children of God.

It is one of the most endearing characteristics of Vaughan's religious verse that he so perfectly realizes the liberating effects of true faith. Through all the doubts and fears he expresses about his own capacity to respond, and despite his awareness that stern judgement for past wickedness rests with Almighty God, the journey of faith is always one which finally leads to the freedom of the spirit. And nowhere does he express it better than in this poem.

Vaughan then turns to the means by which the Christ-like qualities of righteousness, peace and love, which alone can make us free, are to be realized. Only the possession of true humility will enable this state to be brought about:

> Grant I may soft and lowly be,
> And minde those things I cannot see;
> Tye me to faith, though above reason,
> Who question power, they speak treason:
> Let me thy Ass be onely wise
> To carry, not search mysteries;
> Who carries thee, is by thee lead,
> Who argues, follows his own head.
>
> (p. 518, ll.17–24)

He builds now upon the symbolism of the Ass which he has already introduced in 'Palm-Sunday'. The Ass, most despised of creatures, not fit even in the states of Judah and Israel for the carrying of important messengers, but only used for the most lowly of tasks, is for Vaughan the complete symbol of humility. The entire thrust of Biblical tradition is that the lowliness and meekness of the Anointed King of Israel was made plain by the fact that He should 'ride upon an ass, and upon a colt, the foal of an ass' (A.V., *Zechariah*,

Ch. 9, v.9). Throughout his poems which treat the holiness and true humility of childhood it is apparent that Vaughan dismisses reason as something we learn as we grow away from childhood, and which finally ensnares us. He now returns to the theme, using this new symbolism of complete obedience to the will of God which can be achieved only by faith, never by reason. The clear implication is that those who attempt to unlock by reason the mystery of the kingdom of God will never do it; only those who proceed by faith, not consciously searching mysteries, will finally be part of that mystery. Upon that paradox the whole of the central section of his poem is based.

There is, as has already been acknowledged, a political dimension to the poem. Vaughan is very conscious that there is no appreciation of true spirituality in his generation; indeed there is a deliberate attempt to suppress 'truth' itself. It is hardly surprising that he chooses 'death' in the sense of resignation from the corruption of the world, when all around him are the results of the vanity of power:

> To check bad motions, keep me still
> Amongst the dead, where thriving ill
> Without his brags and conquests lies,
> And truth (opprest here) gets the prize.
> At all times, whatsoe'r I do,
> Let me not fail to question, who
> Shares in the *act*, and puts me to't?
>
> (p. 518, ll.25–31)

His extreme concern to avoid action which might lead him to associate with unscrupulous agencies, may very well be linked to a similar concern about the 'lure' which was noted in the previous poem and there is an even more explicit reference to it a few lines later:

> If the world offers to me ought,
> That by thy book must not be sought,
> Or though it should be lawful, may
> Prove not expedient for thy way;
> To shun that peril, let thy grace
> Prevail with me to shun the place.
> Let me be wise to please thee still,

And let men call me what they will.

(p. 519, ll.37–44)

The tension between the demands of a temporal authority and militant political power based upon a very narrow sectarianism, on the one hand, and his own reading of the humility of Christ in the gospels on the other, is acute throughout the poem, and Vaughan handles it more openly than in most of the lyrics he wrote.

Finally, there is an end to the conflict within him, at least for the moment. In the last twenty lines of the poem he returns with full strength to Christ-like humility, and uses the symbolism of the ass in the context of a wider vision of the freedom of God's world. It is a passage of very great beauty, one of the most moving he ever wrote, and its most striking quality is the depth and intensity of the personal feeling which underlies idea and image:

When thus thy milde, instructing hand
Findes thy poor *foal* at thy command,
When he from wilde is become wise,
And slights that most, which men most prize;
When all things here to thistles turn
Pricking his lips, till he doth mourn
And hang the head, sighing for those
Pastures of life, where the Lamb goes:

(p. 519, ll.45–52)

The 'wild ass' features prominently in the Books of the Old Testament, and especially in the *Book of Job*, and 'poor foal' renders again the spirit of Zechariah's prophecy. But Vaughan makes of the ass a real character, whom we pity and also love. He does not at this stage press the comparison between himself and the ass, and a major part of the passage's force is that one interprets the ass so exactly within the Biblical tradition and narrative. Then he twists the narrative and begins to give us the substance of the eternal dream. He uses an image which he employs also in 'The Water-fall' which would appear to have been taken direct from the end of the seventh chapter of *Revelation*:[1]

[1] See 'The Water-fall', p. 538, ll.25–26.

For the Lamb which is in the midst of the throne shall feed them, and shall lead them unto living fountains of waters ...

Vaughan then ends the poem with a prophetic vision. At the precise moment when the world has become nothing but thistles, the symbol of ultimate barrenness and waste, he prays that God shall bring release from living death. He uses the term 'captivity' again, but he clearly means not only the political captivity of England but the entire captivity of men's souls to sin.

O then, just then! break or untye
These bonds, this sad captivity,
This leaden state, which men miscal
Being and life, but is dead thrall.
And when (O God!) the Ass is free,
In a state known to none but thee;
O let him by his *Lord* be led,
To living springs, and there be fed
Where light, joy, health and perfect peace
Shut out all pain and each disease;
Where death and frailty are forgotten,
And bones rejoyce, which once were broken!
(p. 519, ll.53–64)

The great intimacy of the picture is surely the key to this final passage. The image of the Ass freed from all the burdens of life, free to drink God's living water is again dependant in part upon the final picture of the seventh chapter of *Revelation*, which has just been discussed. And the last line of the poem is a reminder not only that God himself has broken the bones of man because of man's sin, but that Vaughan's underlying theme is also the misery and bloodshed of the Civil War and the Commonwealth. It has gone on too long; it is time for the broken limbs of a whole nation and people to be healed. He chooses, quite deliberately the Psalmist's famous petition for the mercy and cleansing power of God to heal the distresses of men:

Purge me with hyssop, and I shall be clean; wash me, and I shall be whiter than snow.

Make me to hear joy and gladness; that the bones which thou hast broken may rejoice.
(A.V., *Psalms*, Ch. 51, vv.7–8)

'The Ass' is a superb lyric. It is such a complete experience; it marvellously combines the intimacy of the individual's spiritual life with the tensions and dramas of the political world; it has tenderness, pity and grace. This lyric is not only one of the finest Vaughan ever wrote but arguably one of the most moving of all seventeenth century religious lyrics.

The third of the poems which employs the symbol of the Ass, and the last poem to illustrate Vaughan's treatment of humility, is 'Tears', just fifteen poems before the end of the second part of *Silex Scintillans.* It is again a lyric in which Vaughan places the drama of his own salavation in the context of a vision of eternity.

O when my God, my glory brings
  His white and holy train,
Unto those clear and living *Springs*,
  Where comes no *stain*!

Where all is *light*, and *flowers*, and *fruit*,
  And *joy*, and *rest*,
Make me amongst them ('tis my suit!)
  The last one, and the least.

(p. 526, ll.1–8)

The picture is not based on any one Book of the Bible, though it has echoes of the prophetic books of the Old Testament and again the *Book of Revelation.* The contrast between the majesty of God, symbolized by his 'train', which Vaughan uses in 'The Retreate' and in several other poems, and his own complete unworthiness, is direct and moving. And as he resumes his symbolism of the Ass he achieves a remarkable economy of words, preserving his balance between the Biblical pastoral narrative and prophetic vision:

And when they all are fed, and have
  Drunk of thy living stream,
Bid thy poor Ass (with tears I crave!)
  Drink after them.

(p. 527, ll.9–12)

The simple moral ending, swift, compact and complete, is very reminiscent of Herbert but the visionary element of the lyric, and its personal passion are Vaughan's and Vaughan's alone:

> Thy love claims highest thanks, my sin
>   The lowest pitch:
> But if he pays, who *loves much*, then
>   Thou hast made beggers rich.
>
> (p. 527, ll.13–16)

Looking at the whole range of Vaughan's poetry on the value of simplicity and innocence in the spiritual life, chiefly expressed through the symbol of the new-born infant, but towards the end of his work by the symbolism of the humility and lowliness of the ass, certain points become clear. First, that very few religious poets writing in English have placed such a great emphasis on the value of simplicity and innocence as Vaughan did. Perhaps only Blake compares with him here, in the single-mindedness and sustained power of his treatment of the theme. Secondly, Vaughan appears to be virtually unique among poets of the seventeenth century in the depth and complexity of his understanding of the child as part of the original splendour of God's creation. There is no doubt whatever that his concept of the child lies at the heart of his spiritual vision. Only Traherne, later in the century shares this view to any great extent, and there is neither the detail nor the breadth in his view, which Vaughan attains.

Finally, the extent and quality of his Biblical imagery in the presentation of his view, is remarkable. He ranges widely over many books of the Bible and mingles Biblical sources freely and with great originality and subtlety. But there can be no doubt, either, that his view of the nature of Christ-like innocence and simplicity, and its importance in the spiritual life is finally a visionary statement, and the most telling and frequent of all his sources is obviously the *Book of Revelation*. In the final chapter of this exploration of Henry Vaughan's religious poetry we shall see what place he accords to Revelation in his total view of the nature of life and spiritual reality.

III

'THE OLD WHITE PROPHETS'

Vaughan's preoccupation with Revelation, the making of all things new, has already been made evident, and will be discussed much more completely later. But the essential prerequisite of this newness of life is a full recognition by man of the evils of his former life and a calling back to the righteousness of God. It is therefore no accident that there is a very great emphasis on Prophecy in many of his poems.

Traditionally the prophet was the man, raised up by God Himself, who told men and women individually, and also a whole people, where they had strayed from God's path. Throughout the Old Testament the great prophetic figures had attested to the goodness of God. They had also spoken against evil wherever they found it and contrasted the evil of men with the righteousness of God. Finally, they had warned the Jewish nation of the righteous anger of God, and the Judgement of God upon Men.

In Vaughan's work there are several major prophetic themes. The first is his equation of the story of God in history with the work of the Prophets. The Old Testament patriarchs and prophets are prime evidence of God's intervention in the affairs of men, and illustrate most powerfully the narrative of God's dealings with a large variety of people, over a long period of human history. Secondly there is the idea of the search; usually it is God's search for the soul of man, to bring man to righteousness, and Vaughan illustrates this by reference to the lives and experience of the patriarchs. Occasionally it is man's search for God, in which the Old Testament fathers aid his understanding of the nature of God, and lead him on to personal encounter with Christ. Finally there is the persistent note of the Judgement of God, which is seen as one of the principal tasks of the Prophet.

These three most important ideas are so closely inter-related in his work that it is not valuable to divide his prophetic poems into three categories. It is much more revealing to appreciate how in his imagery and thought he relates these ideas, and also to see whether there is any notable progression, and any difference between the two parts of his work. To do this one must take the poems in their chronological sequence.

'Regeneration' has been judged by a number of critics to be a key poem. It is the very first poem in the book, and certainly contains within it a large number of ideas and images which he explores in later poems. It would also seem to be autobiographical, and the spiritual conflict he depicts within it may not be so far different from Vaughan's own spiritual struggle, which led directly to the writing of *Silex Scintillans.* More important for our present purpose it is directly influenced by Old Testament prophecy and defines clearly an important part of Vaughan's concern with the Biblical prophets.

'Regeneration' is also one of the poems which is concerned quite specifically with a search, and the imagery of the first stanza gives us the spiritual climate which caused the search, and accompanied the first stages of the journey:

It was high-spring, and all the way
  Primros'd, and hung with shade;
  Yet, was it frost within,
    And surly winds
Blasted my infant buds, and sinne
  Like Clouds ecclips'd my mind.

(p. 397, ll.3–8)

The 'Pilgrims Eye' of the second stanza (1.13) introduces the note of determined spiritual quest, and the entire structure, thought and imagery of the third stanza announces a judgement, which, though it is not final, is sufficiently dramatic and decisive to give a desperate urgency of personal quest to the stanzas which follow:

So sigh'd I upwards still, at last
    'Twixt steps, and falls
I reach'd the pinacle, where plac'd
  I found a paire of scales,
  I tooke them up and layd
    In th'one late paines,
The other smoake, and pleasures weigh'd
  But prov'd the heavier graines;

(p. 397, ll.17–24)

It is at this point, immediately after the discovery of the truth about his own condition, that the pilgrim begins to relive some of the most powerful and climatic moments of Old Testament experience. The inference seems to be that only by seeking aid from those who had a direct experience of God, and one which dramatically changed their lives, is the pilgrim able to make any progress in his spiritual journey:

> With that, some cryed, *Away*; straight I
> Obey'd, and led
> Full East, a faire, fresh field could spy
> Some call'd it, *Jacobs Bed*;
> A Virgin-soile, which no
> Rude feet ere trod,
> Where (since he stept there,) only go
> Prophets, and friends of God.
>
> (p. 397, ll.25–32)

Vaughan uses Jacob in very much the same way he used Isaac in '*Isaacs* Marriage', as a central figure in the history of the Jewish people and also as a Patriarch who was able to see with great and clear vision the purposes of the Almighty, once his life had been changed by personal encounter. It is important to recognize that Vaughan does not differentiate to any great extent between patriarch and prophet. The Church's 'fathers', such as Abraham, Isaac and Jacob, are treated as men who acted under God's divine instruction and therefore as one with the prophets, even though they were not officially designated as prophets. And Jacob in this poem has an even greater spiritual weight and significance than Isaac in '*Isaacs* Marriage' in that his was a life not so consecrated from the first but changed miraculously on a journey by the direct intervention of God. The parallel with Vaughan's own situation must be noted, because he makes so very much of it in the poem itself. The very name of Jacob – 'God rewards' contains a promise to the pilgrim who also treads Jacob's way, and the intimacy of the personal relationship which God had with him is emphasized not only by the use of 'Jacobs Bed' but also by the very personal nature of the image which closes the stanza – 'friends of God'.

In this, the first of the many Old Testament pictures which Vaughan gives us in *Silex Scintillans*, he fuses two distinct meanings. At the place where Jacob lodged for the night he was given the direct promise of God:

> And, behold, the Lord stood above it, and said, I am the Lord God of Abraham thy father, and the God of Isaac: the land whereon thou liest, to thee will I give it, and to thy seed:
>
> And thy seed shall be as the dust of the earth, and thou shalt spread abroad to the west, and to the east, and to the north, and to the south: and in thee and in thy seed shall all families of the earth be blessed.
>
> (A. V., *Genesis*, Ch. 28, vv.13–14)

Vaughan's pilgrim is thus given a sign of the promised land, even as Jacob was, and enters into that contract with God by having seen the hallowed place where God met with Jacob and blessed him.

But Beth-el is also a precise geographical location, and this has been emphasized by several of the Old Testament prophets, most notably Hosea, and it is the intimacy of man meeting God directly which fascinates Henry Vaughan. Hosea's description of the meeting catches absolutely the sense which is in Vaughan's lines:

> Yea, he had power over the angel, and prevailed: he wept, and made supplication unto him: he found him in Beth-el, and there he spake with us;
>
> (A. V., *Hosea*, Ch. 12 v.4)

In this place of promise and sacred commitment where a man such as Jacob, who knew both good and evil in his former life, had seen God, Vaughan seems to reach a turning point in his own pilgrimage. He casts his eye upon a grove and expresses his delight in a landscape which combines both the landscape he knew and the Biblical country he imagined:

> Here, I repos'd; but scarse well set,
> A grove descryed
> Of stately height, whose branches met
> And mixt on every side;
> I entred, and once in

(Amaz'd to see't,)
Found all was chang'd, and a new spring
Did all my senses greet;

(p. 398, ll.33–40)

The other outstanding prophetic symbol in 'Regeneration' is that of the wind, with which he closes the poem, and Vaughan introduces here a technique which becomes familiar in his work as a whole, and particularly in the poems of prophecy. He deliberately unites the great prophetic messages of the Old Testament with those of the New. The wind is of course very widely used, throughout the Old Testament, as a symbol of God's spirit and a clear sign of the sacred presence. Sometimes God sends the wind as his agent; at other times he rides upon the wind, as in the famous instance in the song of David:

He bowed the heavens also, and came down; and darkness was upon his feet.

And he rode upon a cherub, and did fly; and he was seen upon the wings of the wind.

(A. V., 2 *Samuel*, Ch. 22, vv.10–11)

Frequently God's message is given in the wind to the Holy Prophet, as it was to Ezekiel, and then communicated to the people. When the wind is used as a prophetic instrument of God's will the clear implication is that it must be obeyed. It is a thing of irresistible power, exactly as Vaughan characterizes it in the penultimate stanza of his poem:

Here musing long, I heard
A rushing wind
Which still increas'd, but whence it stirr'd
No where I could not find;

(p. 399, ll.69–72)

But Vaughan was certainly conscious of the central importance of the wind in New Testament symbolism, and especially the words attributed to Christ in the story of Nicodemus, narrated in the *Gospel of John*:

Marvel not that I said unto thee, Ye must be born again.

The wind bloweth where it listeth, and thou hearest the sound thereof, but canst not tell whence it cometh, and whither it goeth: so is every one that is born of the Spirit.

(A. V., *John*, Ch. 3, vv.7–8)

It is an exact and most conclusive end to the poem. The pilgrimage which began in order that he might find himself, is transformed when he is allowed to tread where Jacob trod and found the Almighty. And the prophetic wind which speaks the words of God directly to man is, by Christ's own definition, bound by nothing else on earth, so that any man, however unworthy, can be quickened by it, and be re-born.

So, in this very first poem of the collection Vaughan has used the central theme of Man's search for God, and also the search of the Spirit of God for the soul of man. He has also introduced as a subsidiary theme God's direct intervention in human affairs, by his choice of Jacob's vision. Of prophetic judgement there is nothing specific, though he implies throughout the poem that the pilgrim is driven on his search because he is aware of the abiding judgement of God.

'Day of Judgement', only three poems later, reveals an entirely different aspect of prophecy. Here Vaughan is centrally concerned with prophetic judgement and the prophecy is set in apocalyptic terms, which would seem to be derived directly from specific Biblical visions.

The poem's opening has all the drama and urgency of a final warning, and uses all the elements of the world in its complex picture of violence and destruction:

> When through the North a fire shall rush
> And rowle into the East,
> And like a firie torrent brush
> And sweepe up *South*, and *West*,
>
> When all shall streame, and lighten round
> And with surprizing flames
> Both stars, and Elements confound
> And quite blot out their names,
>
> (p. 402, ll.1–8)

The first stanza seems to be influenced in general terms by Christ's vision of the end of the world, and the ensuing judgement of God, when he predicts that 'they shall come from the east, and from the west, and from the north, and from the south, and shall sit down in the kingdom of God' (A. V., *Luke*, Ch. 13, v.29). Whether this was the actual source is not important, but it is clearly an apocalyptic vision in New Testament terms, and it is extremely unlikely that Vaughan would not have been very familiar with so famous a pronouncement as this. But the details of the fire which shall destroy the universe as we know it, which he gives in the second stanza, do correspond fairly closely with the vision of Peter. Vaughan has given as his text a verse from the first epistle of Peter but the vision of fire is in a celebrated passage from the second epistle:

> But the day of the Lord will come as a thief in the night; in the which the heavens shall pass away with a great noise, and the elements shall melt with fervent heat, the earth also and the works that are therein shall be burned up.
> (A. V., 2 *Peter*, Ch. 3, v.10)

It is all sufficiently near the epistle to be a fairly literal translation of Biblical images and ideas, but Vaughan, as has been amply illustrated elsewhere, seldom keeps to one Biblical source. Part of his poetic art is that he can range widely over relevant material. The fourth stanza, for example, with its prophecy that the very heavens will cease to be:

> When like a scrowle the heavens shal passe
> And vanish cleane away,
> And nought must stand of that vast space
> Which held up night, and day,
> (p. 403, ll.13–16)

owes a good deal to one of the visions of *Revelation*:

> And the heaven departed as a scroll when it is rolled together; and every mountain and island were moved out of their places.
> (A. V., *Revelation*, Ch. 6, v.14)

The next stanza with its prophecy of 'one lowd blast' which shall call forth the dead to rise, recalls the well-known Pauline vision in the last part of the fifteenth chapter of 1 *Corinthians*, but for the judgement of God Vaughan returns to *Revelation*, and also to the first epistle of Peter. The God whom he here describes is the One who appears in solemn majesty to preside over an enormous trial of all the people on earth:

> When thou shalt make the Clouds thy seate,
> And in the open aire

The Quick, and dead, both small and great
Must to thy barre repaire;

(p. 403, ll.21–24)

The image of God seated upon a cloud follows closely the imagery of the fourteenth chapter of *Revelation*, a source which Vaughan uses to such marked effect in so many of his visionary passages. In this case it is an angel, appearing in the likeness of Christ, who acts as Divine agent:

> And I looked, and behold a white cloud, and upon the cloud one sat like unto the Son of man, having on his head a golden crown, and in his hand a sharp sickle.
>
> (A. V., *Revelation*, Ch. 14, v.14)

The picture of 'the Quick, and dead' appearing for judgement is contained in Peter's denunciation of the wicked, only two verses before the text on which Vaughan has based his poem:

> Who shall give account to him that is ready to judge the quick and the dead.
>
> (A. V., 1 *Peter*, Ch. 4, vv.4–5)

This powerful apocalyptic vision which Vaughan has derived from the prophetic passages which close the New Testament, gives great urgency to the message of the last four stanzas of the poem, that only suffering here and now will kill the sin in him and keep him repentant. And the most important word here is surely 'Prepare'. It is time to act now, to sweep away the evil of his former life:

Prepare, prepare me then, O God!
And let me now begin
To feele my loving fathers *Rod*
Killing the man of sinne!

(p. 403, ll.29–32)

He chooses deliberately a word of great prophetic significance, taken as it is from one of the most celebrated prophecies of Isaiah:

> The voice of him that crieth in the wilderness, Prepare ye the way of the Lord, make straight in the desert a highway for our God.
>
> (A. V., *Isaiah*, Ch. 40, v.3)

This is later echoed in various ways by all the gospel writers, and forms one entire section of Scripture, the movement towards repentance under the prophetic judgement of God.

In 'Day of Judgement' Vaughan has again linked Old and New Testament prophecy, as he did in 'Regeneration'. He has also provided a fuller picture of the end of the world than in any other of his prophetic poems, but it is notable that he has not widened his theme to include specifically the Puritan perpetrators of wickedness and murder, as he does in the second poem of this title, in the last part of *Silex Scintillans*. He is content to declare his enmity to what he terms 'the world', and upon that to rest the continuity of his faith:

> A living *FAITH*, a *HEART* of flesh,
>   The *WORLD* an Enemie,
> This last will keepe the first two fresh,
>   And bring me, where I'de be.
>
> (p. 403, ll.41–44)

'Religion' is significant in revealing his political attitude, as we saw earlier, but is also enormously important as a prophetic statement which draws widely and deeply upon both the historical and prophetic books of the Bible. It is interesting that it follows immediately upon 'Day of Judgement' and at least in its insistence upon the Judgement of God is similar to the previous poem. But its primary importance is that it considerably develops the theme of God's intimate conversation with man which Vaughan began in 'Regeneration'.

The first two verses of this poem contain clear references to the vision of the Angel in the first chapter of the prophet, *Zechariah*, but it is characteristic of Vaughan that he has used images which occur in other parts of the Old Testament too, so that he mingles the visionary insights and also the prophetic utterances:

> My God, when I walke in those groves,
> And leaves thy spirit still doth fan,
> I see in each shade that there growes
> An Angell talking with a man.
>
> Under a *Juniper*, some house,

Or the coole *Mirtles* canopie,
Others beneath an *Oakes* greene boughs,
Or at some *Fountaines* bubling Eye;

(p. 404, ll.1–8)

Vaughan's choice of Zechariah's prophecy is deliberate; it concerned the Lord's displeasure with Jerusalem and Judah, and whether it was possible to save them. Vaughan was clearly drawing the same lesson and 'Jerusalem' becomes his own land, controlled by the Puritans. Can it be saved? His answer seems to be that only the direct intervention of God can save it.

> Then said I, O my lord, what are these? and the angel that talked with me said unto me, I will shew thee what these be.
> And the man that stood among the myrtle trees answered and said, They are those whom the Lord hath sent to walk to and fro through the earth.
>
> (A. V., *Zechariah*, Ch. 1, vv.9–10)

But the prophecy, though it has an obvious political significance, is of a general importance. Though much of the first stanza and the 'Mirtles' of the second have their source clearly in Zechariah's vision, Vaughan's use of groves in the first line and 'Oakes' in the third line of the second stanza widen the historical scope. Indeed the grove, one of his most frequent terms, is nothing less than the place where the Spirit of God is both invoked and felt, and it is marked out for special significance from the first book of the Bible onwards through many of the prophets. The reason is clear; it signifies both the birth of the Jewish nation and the beginning of God's communication with man, through his servant Abraham:

> And Abraham planted a grove in Beer-sheba, and called there on the name of the Lord, the everlasting God.
>
> (A. V., *Genesis*, Ch. 21, v.33)

Vaughan thus establishes from the beginning that it is the intimacy and directness of God's bond with man that is vital in human affairs. And he continues the theme by a series of images. The Juniper gives a picture of Elijah in the worst moments of his life, hunted by Jezebel:

> And as he lay and slept under a juniper tree, behold, then an angel touched him, and said unto him, Arise and eat.
>
> (A. V., 1 *Kings*, Ch. 19, v.5)

The 'Mirtle' of Zechariah's vision provides a contrast, for here the Angel takes the initiative, but the intimacy and importance of God's intervention is similar. And the 'Oakes green boughs' gives us yet another example of the way in which God called Gideon to be both Judge and prophet:

> And there came an angel of the Lord, and sat under an oak which was in Ophrah, ...
>
> And the angel of the Lord appeared unto him, and said unto him, The Lord is with thee, thou mighty man of valour.
>
> (A. V., *Judges*, Ch. 6, vv.11–12)

The concentration of Biblical images, each summoning up a different example of God's ability to intervene directly in the affairs of his own people has a double effect. First it has the advantage of intensifying the argument and creating an obvious climax. But secondly it gives us clear and rapid contrasts. The great contrast between the '*fountaines* bubling Eye' and 'Here *Jacob* dreames', for example, is most marked, and the beauty of the contrasting pictures in the third and fourth stanzas is a remarkable feature of the power and colour of Vaughan's writings:

> Here *Jacob* dreames, and wrestles; there
> *Elias* by a Raven is fed,
> Another time by th'Angell, where
> He brings him water with his bread;
>
> In *Abr'hams* Tent the winged guests
> (O how familiar then was heaven!)
> Eate, drinke, discourse, sit downe, and rest
> Untill the Coole, and shady *Even*;
>
> (p. 404, ll.9–16)

Sufficient reference has already been made to the significance of Jacob's meeting with God, in 'Regeneration'. It is an incident Vaughan could never forget; he returns to it again and again in his poetry. But the salvation of Elijah is just as remarkable and interestingly Vaughan gives us two instances of it, the one of the juniper already discussed, and the earlier episode of Elijah's escape to the brook Cherith:

> And the ravens brought him bread and flesh in the morning, and bread and flesh in the evening; and he drank of the brook.
>
> (A. V., 1 *Kings*, Ch. 17, v.6)

The fifth stanza in fact sums up the entire story of God's dealings with individual men. Vaughan has saved the illustration which gives him the broadest possible base until the last. Here is an incident which shows how the messengers of God not only treat their chosen servants with direct intimacy, but even familiarly, as friends or family. There are a number of occasions when Vaughan sees Heaven stooping so close to earth that the two become almost one. This is such an experience:

> And the Lord appeared unto him in the plains of Mamre: and he sat in the tent door in the heat of the day;
>
> And he lift up his eyes and looked, and lo, three men stood by him: and when he saw them, he ran to meet them from the tent door, and bowed himself toward the ground.
>
> (A. V., *Genesis*, Ch. 18, vv.1–2)

Nor should one overlook the context of Vaughan's source. He is far too conscious and deliberate an artist not to have been aware that this intimate conversation between Abraham and the messengers of God is part of God's prophetic judgement upon the sin of men in general and the wickedness of Sodom and Gomorrah in particular. God speaks to his righteous servants in friendship, and intimacy, but the burden of the prophetic message is not blunted: the wicked who will not give up their ways will finally be destroyed.

But the prophecy is not only one of judgement; at the positive level it is the continuing promise that the Spirit of God is available to his servants, and Vaughan's own need of intimate communion with God, and his plea that his life shall be touched by the same Spirit which moved the early fathers, is a vital part of the latter part of the poem, and especially the sixth stanza:

> Nay thou thy selfe, my God, in *fire*,
> *Whirle–winds*, and *Clouds*, and the *soft voice*
> Speak'st there so much, that I admire
> We have no Conf'rence in these daies;
>
> (p. 404, ll.17–20)

The stanza is based directly upon the very famous episode in which the angel of the Lord comforts Elijah and God Himself is heard, after earthquake, wind and fire, in 'the still small voice' (A. V., 1 *Kings*, Ch. 19, vv.11–12).

The final aspect of 'Religion' which is worthy of note is that Vaughan does not stop at the level of Old Testament history and prophecy. The remainder of the poem contains, in addition to the sharp political comment already discussed, the assertion that Christ, far from negating the work of the prophets, enriches it, by the miracles of his early ministry (the water changed to wine), and by his willingness to save the world, though he is Son of God. To the message of 'the old white prophets' has been joined the Messianic message of Christ.

This is, without any question, one of Vaughan's finest poems, sadly neglected by the anthologies. It is a remarkably direct declaration of Christian truth and also an exact definition of the prophetic role of the Church itself, as Vaughan believes it should be. And there are few finer examples in *Silex Scintillans* of his ability to combine a large number of Old and New Testament sources in order to press home his theme of the importance of man's intimate communion with God.

It would appear that Vaughan was much impressed by the significance of Prophecy in the early part of his work in *Silex Scintillans*. To some extent his interest changes later in the work, although the general influence of prophetic utterance upon his thought remains. Immediately after 'Religion' is placed 'The Search', which is another superb illustration of the central importance of the prophetic message. It is the third lyric in sequence in which he has used this theme.

'The Search' differs from 'Religion' in that its first and dominant note is the New Testament account of Christ's life. The focal point of the first twenty lines is the birth and early life of Jesus, but as in 'Regeneration' Vaughan uses the idea of a spiritual journey, in which he, the pilgrim, seeks his living Lord. There are, in fact, several echoes of 'Regeneration' in the poem but there is a greater lyrical intensity in the imagery:

'Tis now cleare day: I see a Rose
Bud in the bright East, and disclose
The Pilgrim-Sunne; all night have I
Spent in a roving Extasie
To find my Saviour; I have been
As far as *Bethlem*, and have seen
His Inne, and Cradle; Being there
I met the *Wise-men*, askt them where
He might be found, or what starre can
Now point him out, grown up a Man?
To *Egypt* hence I fled, ran o're
All her parcht bosome to *Nile's* shore
Her yearly nurse;

(p. 405, ll.1–13)

Quite apart from the beautiful and clear image of the 'Pilgrim-Sunne' and very strong personal note of excitement of 'roving Extasie' which seem to set the places of Christ's early life almost in Vaughan's own native landscape, there is a very deliberate echoing of ancient Jewish history. Vaughan could have treated 'Egypt' as merely the refuge of Christ from his enemies, but the Nile imagery has linked the infant Moses with the infant Christ. The earlier leader and prophet and first statesman of the Jewish nation sees now his promise richly fulfilled by the coming of Christ.

In the middle section of the poem Vaughan considerably develops this theme of Christ as the fulfilment of Old Testament prophecy, and once again the images show an extraordinary depth of Biblical knowledge and also a great technical ingenuity. One passage is worth quoting in some detail:

Tyr'd here, I came to *Sychar*; thence
To *Jacobs wel*, bequeathed since
Unto his sonnes, (where often they
In those calme, golden Evenings lay
Watring their flocks, and having spent
Those white dayes, drove home to the Tent
Their *well-fleec'd* traine;) And here (O fate!)
I sit, where once my Saviour sate;
The angry Spring in bubbles swell'd
Which broke in sighes still, as they fill'd,
And whisper'd *Jesus had been there*

But *Jacobs children would not heare.*
(p. 406, ll.21–32)

Returning again to his favourite subject of Jacob, he provides in this passage a most intimate picture of the land which Jacob bequeathed to his children near to the Samarian city of Sychar. Through this image of pastoral contentment and peace he conveys the fact that the promise of God had been fulfilled in the life of Jacob, and is now passed on to his children. The fulfilment of God's prophecy of peace and blessedness is in 'those calme, golden Evenings', and Vaughan's use of 'white dayes' re-enforces the idea of the holiness of those who do God's will. Finally 'Tent', which in Old Testament terms is the only permanence of the nomad's life, suggests that in their only dwelling place they are intimate with God. The entire passage is rich in Old Testament reference and allusion.

But Jesus also went to Sychar, and Vaughan now carefully supplements the Old Testament prophecy of God's promise, by the New Testament's insistence that Christ not only fulfils the prophets, but goes beyond them in offering man a new Covenant. And though the Jews, as he indicates, reject Him, Christ's promise to the woman of Samaria is that he will give to all who accept Him 'a well of water springing up into everlasting life' (A. V., *John*, Ch. 4, v.14). Indeed the woman, after enquiring whether Jesus is 'greater than our father Jacob' (v.12) recognizes Him as 'a prophet' (v.19).

There is a further picture of Christ in the poem, in which Vaughan again combines both parts of the Bible to illustrate the heroic and prophetic elements of Christ's mission. Frustrated thus far, his Pilgrim thinks of searching for Christ in the wilderness:

He liv'd there safe, 'twas his retreat
From the fierce *Jew*, and *Herods* heat,
And forty dayes withstood the fell,
And high temptations of hell;
With Seraphins there talked he
His fathers flaming ministrie,
He heavn'd their *walks*, and with his eyes
Made those wild shades a Paradise,
(p. 406, ll.55–62)

There is a particular feature of this passage which shows Vaughan at his finest. It is the clarity and concentration of his Biblical insight. His reference to the 'Seraphins' is a master stroke of invention which immediately conveys the importance of Christ as not only the Son of God, but also the last and greatest of the prophets. The seraphim were those angels of God who declared His Holiness in the courts of Heaven, and Vaughan knows full well what part they played in the calling of the prophet Isaiah, and how they gave majesty and awe to the entire prophetic calling and ministry:

> each one had six wings; with twain he covered his face, and with twain he covered his feet, and with twain he did fly.
>
> And one cried unto another and said, Holy, holy, holy is the Lord of hosts: the whole earth is full of his glory.
>
> (A. V., *Isaiah*, Ch. 6, vv.2–3)

The name of these Seraphins was 'the burning ones', and Vaughan clearly intends to convey, by his term 'flaming ministers', the supreme spiritual illumination which enabled Christ to defeat the powers of Hell. Christ is clothed with all the prophetic majesty of God.

But 'The Search' is in no sense a mere recital of Biblical history. By using the device of the pilgrimage, he has given the poem a dramatic urgency and power. And though he has illuminated the great message of the prophets, fulfilled now in Christ, he has done so with an intimacy and deep sense of personal involvement, which is extremely rare in English religious poetry. And in the song which closes the poem he returns, as he has done in 'Regeneration', to the Spirit of God which alone can give meaning and point to the religious life. The pilgrimage ends not here on earth, but in the discovery of a world which lies beyond this world of historical event and transitory experience:

> To rack old Elements,
>   or Dust
>   and say
> Sure here he must
>   needs stay
> Is not the way,
>   nor just.

Search well another world; who studies this,
Travels in Clouds, seeks *Manna*, where none is.
(p. 407, ll.88–96)

And by his use of '*Manna*' in the final line he has made clear that this fruit which God provided for the needs of his people on earth must now be considered as spiritual sustenance available only to those who can look beyond this present world.

It is very interesting that after this trilogy of poems which is based substantially upon Biblical prophecy Vaughan's use of the prophets, though still important, becomes much less frequent in his work.

In 'Midnight', however, much later in the collection, his reflection upon the glory of the night sky leads him briefly to an apocalyptic vision which reminds one of 'Day of Judgement'.

Thy heav'ns (some say,)
Are a firie-liquid light,
Which mingling aye
Streames, and flames thus to the sight.
(p. 421, ll.17–20)

There are general influences of the *Second Epistle of Peter* here, as in the previous poem, but Vaughan seems also to be recalling the vivid cry of Isaiah's prophecy:

Oh that thou wouldest rend the heavens, that thou wouldest come down, that the mountains might flow down at thy presence.

As when the melting fire burneth, the fire that causeth the waters to boil, to make thy name known to thine adversaries, that the nations may tremble at thy presence!
(Ch. 64, vv.1–2)

This apocalyptic vision of the prophetic message prefaces Vaughan's own deep and intimate cry for the coming upon him of the spirit of God, and once again it is the personal intensity, the desire for a private vision of the power and majesty of God's presence which characterize the thought and imagery of his lines:

Come then, my god!
Shine on this bloud,

And water in one beame,
And thou shalt see
Kindled by thee
Both liquors burne, and streame.
O what bright quicknes,
Active brightnes,
And celestiall flowes
Will follow after
On that water,
Which thy spirit blowes!

(p. 421, ll.21–32)

There are only two other poems in the first part of *Silex Scintillans* in which Vaughan makes direct mention of the Old Testament narrative of God's dealings with men, and they follow one another, towards the end of the collection. In the first, 'The Pilgrimage', the references are brief, but nonetheless worthy of note.

As the title suggests, man's spiritual journey is again the main subject of the poem, and the stars of night are once more the companions of this pilgrimage. Swiftly and confidently Vaughan returns to the story of Jacob:

Then *Jacob*-like lodge in a place
(A place, and no more, is set down,)
Where till the day restore the race
They rest and dream homes of their own.

(p. 464, ll.5–8)

What follows is a most poignant lament for the security of God's presence. Although Jacob had the brilliance of the vision, the night which revealed it was spent by the wayside, far from home. It is strange that until the very last stanza of the poem there is no mention of Christ, or of Christ's historic mission to bring people home to the righteousness of God, so prominent a feature of prophecy. Instead Vaughan uses, as often in his religious poetry, general images of Nature:

As Birds rob'd of their native wood,
Although their Diet may be fine,
Yet neither sing, nor like their food,
But with the thought of home do pine;

(p. 464, ll.17–20)

At the end, however, he returns to the Biblical message, and includes Christ in his final image:

> O feed me then! and since I may
> Have yet more days, more nights to Count,
> So strengthen me, Lord, all the way,
> That I may travel to thy Mount.
>
> (p. 465, ll.25–28)

Mount Zion, the home of all God's people, is surely coupled with the Mount of Olives, which Vaughan takes as his subject just a few poems later in the collection. And once again the great prophetic message of man's deep necessity for a return to the righteousness of God is completed by the fullness of the revelation which Christ brought by his sacrifice.

'The Law, and the Gospel', which follows 'The Pilgrimage', is a fascinating and quite major statement of prophetic themes, and deserves detailed study. It contains both traditional prophetic statement, following the Old Testament closely and in depth, and also elements of Vaughan's own prophetic vision of the nature of life and the role of God in history.

The first stanza is a vivid and direct account of the way in which God dealt with the stubbornness of the people of Israel, and by the giving of his law on Mount Sinai, made them chastened and obedient to his will. God's servant Moses is not directly mentioned but the fierceness and power of the prophetic message is everywhere made clear:

> Lord, when thou didst on *Sinai* pitch
> And shine from *Paran*, when a firie Law
> Pronounc'd with thunder, and thy threats did thaw
> Thy Peoples hearts, when all thy weeds were rich
> And Inaccessible for light,
> Terrour, and might,
> How did poor flesh (which after thou didst weare,)
> Then faint, and fear!
> Thy Chosen flock, like leafs in a high wind,
> Whisper'd obedience, and their heads Inclin'd.
>
> (p. 465, ll.1–10)

The images of the weeds, and 'leafs in a high wind', and 'the threatening Clouds' in the second stanza (l.15) are all in

Vaughan's most confident manner, and his continual contrast of the two Mounts dramatizes the poem's main argument, which is not dissimilar to the one he used in 'Religion' – that people who proclaim their faith in the Christ of the gospels forget the majesty of the law of God:

> We Climb up this, and have too all the way
> Thy hand our stay,
> Nay, thou tak'st ours, and (which ful Comfort brings)
> Thy Dove too bears us on her sacred wings.
>
> (p. 465, ll.17–20)

But even the Spirit of God, symbolized by the Holy Dove, is not enough to keep the heart clean. The tremendous emphasis which Vaughan places upon the Law is perhaps the clearest single piece of evidence for his interpretation of the Prophets as central to an understanding of God. The prophets revealed the Law as the strongest bond between God and man, the eternal covenant established on the Sacred Mount, and it is Vaughan's view that nothing can supplant it. And although he takes the argument at a doctrinal level he is making a point which would appear to be still at the core of the Christian Faith:

> O plant in me thy *Gospel*, and thy *Law*,
> Both *Faith*, and *Awe*;
> So twist them in my heart, that ever there
> I may as wel as *Love*, find too thy *fear*!
>
> (p. 465, ll.27–30)

The great urgency, almost desperation, of the final stanza may well have been occasioned by his memory of the Civil War, and especially the terrible shedding of blood.

> Let me not spil, but drink thy bloud,
> Not break thy fence, and by a black Excess
> Force down a Just Curse, when thy hands would bless;
> Let me not scatter, and despise my food,
> Or nail those blessed limbs again
> Which bore my pain;
>
> (p. 466, ll.31–36)

seems to echo several of the poems which express grief and fear at Puritan excesses, and especially 'Christs Nativity'.

'The Law, and the Gospel' not only combines the prophetic messages of the Old and New Testaments, but also attests to the role of God in human history, and His entire relationship with His people, as the prophets have revealed it. It is also, however, a prophetic statement of the Judgement of God, most succinctly contained in the poem's final lines:

> So Shall thy mercies flow: for while I fear,
>   I know, thou'lt bear,
> But should thy mild Injunction nothing move me,
> I would both think, and Judge I did not love thee.
>
> (p. 466, ll.37–40)

Occurring, as it does, almost at the end of the first part of *Silex Scintillans* it is in many ways a fitting summary of his attitude to the Old Testament in general, and his treatment of Prophecy in particular, in this entire section of his work.

It is noticeable that there are fewer poems which deal directly with the Patriarchs and prophets in the second part of his work. The changing social and political climate in Britain in the early 1650's certainly seems to have influenced his choice of subject. There are far more poems expressing horror at the bloodshed and bitterness of the Civil War period and its immediate aftermath; there are more poems which plead the necessity for personal forgiveness and greater piety of life.

However, there are still lyrics which are based directly on Biblical incidents, and there is a continued emphasis upon God's role in human history, and especially upon His place as Righteous Judge. Indeed, the note of prophetic judgement, which we have observed in the first part, becomes even sharper and more insistent in the second. There is also the reminder that Christ is the fulfilment of the prophetic message. The group of Ascension poems which begins the second part is much concerned with this general theme. Two of these lyrics, 'Ascension-day' and 'White Sunday' deserve particular mention here; the others will be discussed in detail in the final chapter.

'Ascension-day', as its name suggests, is an evocation of the spirit of the risen Lord, and it is also a reminder of several of his earlier lyrics in that Vaughan presents it as a personal pilgrimage in which he searches ecstatically for his Saviour. The freshness and spontaneity of the nature images should also be noted. Christ is risen, and here is the world made new for every pilgrim:

> I greet thy Sepulchre, salute thy Grave,
> That blest inclosure, where the Angels gave
> The first glad tidings of thy early light,
> And resurrection from the earth and night.
> I see that morning in thy Converts tears,
> Fresh as the dew, which but this dawning wears?
> I smell her spices, and her ointment yields,
> As rich a scent as the now Primros'd-fields:
>
> (p. 481, ll.15–22)

Secondly, the poem contains a most moving and beautiful sustained image of 'Saints and Angels', the holy messengers of God. This passage is remarkable not only for the feeling of intense spiritual exaltation it creates, but also for the intimacy with which Vaughan describes the mediation of these messengers. He claims to see them directly and as if in an extraordinary ecstacy he describes this unique experience in which he was privileged to become virtually a part of this secret communion between these holy ones of God. There is a great majesty in his communication of this vision, which is expressed not only in the image but also in the exalted rhythm of his lines:

> What stirs, what posting intercourse and mirth
> Of Saints and Angels glorifie the earth?
> What sighs, what whispers, busie stops and stays;
> Private and holy talk fill all the ways?
> They pass as at the last great day, and run
> In their white robes to seek the risen Sun;
> I see them, hear them, mark their haste, and move
> Amongst them, with them, wing'd with faith and love.
>
> (p. 481, ll.25–32)

Another notable feature of the poem is the extent to which Vaughan has fused Christ's life with the original splendour of the world as revealed in the first chapter of 'Genesis'. The promise of God, through his holy prophets, is absolutely fulfilled in Christ, and Vaughan's own sense of wonder and awe, as the delighted pilgrim, is in the prophecy made true. There is an excitement and great innocence in these lines which characterize Vaughan at his best:

> I walk the fields of *Bethani* which shine
> All now as fresh as *Eden*, and as fine.
> Such was the bright world, on the first seventh day,
> Before man brought forth sin, and sin decay;
> When like a Virgin clad in *Flowers* and *green*
> The pure earth sat, and the fair woods had seen
> No frost, but flourish'd in that youthful vest,
> With which their great Creator had them drest:
>
> (p. 482, ll.37–44)

Finally, Christ Himself is characterized as a prophetic figure. He has not only fulfilled the promises declared in the Old Testament; he has added a new dimension by giving to all people a fresh opportunity to return to God:

> I see him leading out his chosen Train,
> All sad with tears, which like warm Summer-rain
> In silent drops steal from their holy eyes,
> Fix'd lately on the Cross, now on the skies.
>
> (p. 482, ll.51–54)

Vaughan's use of 'Train' has already been discussed. Certainly the most dramatic use of it in the Old Testament, in Isaiah's prophecy (*Isaiah*, Ch. 6), would seem to be the sense in which he employs it here too, and it denotes, as in the prophecy, all the great majesty of God himself. But it also denotes the followers of Christ; those who mourned with Him and now rejoice at his victory. The exquisite tenderness and delicacy of the 'tears ... like warm Summer-rain' give exactly the right touch of sadness. However, one must not overlook that the poem ends with the absolute necessity for Judgement of the world. Christ the Saviour may be the One whom the pilgrim searches to find, but the divine prophecy is also one of the Judgement of God. For Vaughan, as a believer, Christ ascendent and triumphant at the right hand of God is finally Christ the Judge of all:

> The cloud doth now receive thee, and their sight
> Having lost thee, behold two men in white!

Two and no more: *what two attest, is true*,
Was thine own answer to the stubborn Jew.
Come then thou faithful witness! come dear Lord
Upon the Clouds again to judge this world!
(p. 482, ll.57–62)

'Ascension-day' is an intensely personal expression of mature faith, superbly expressed. It is without doubt one of his greatest lyrics.

In the fourth and last of the 'Ascension' poems, 'White Sunday', Vaughan returns to the theme of prophetic judgement. We have already discussed the ways in which he uses much of the poem to deliver his own judgement upon the Puritan rulers who held sway at that time. But it should also be noted that Vaughan sees the whole of Ascension-tide as part of the prophetic mission and role of the Church. Indeed, he specially adds prophecy to the original description given in 'Acts':

And there appeared unto them cloven tongues like as of fire, and it sat upon each of them.

And they were all filled with the Holy Ghost, and began to speak with other tongues, as the Spirit gave them utterance.
((A. V., *Acts*, Ch. 2, vv.3–4)

Vaughan's interpretation of this is in the second stanza of the poem:

Those flames which on the Apostles rush'd
At this great feast, and in a tyre
Of cloven Tongues their heads all brush'd,
And crown'd them with Prophetic fire:
(p. 485, ll.5–8)

Then, after his denunciation of what he believes to be Puritan hypocrisy he completes the poem with two Old Testament references of particular significance:

O come! refine us with thy fire!
Refine us! we are at a loss.
Let not thy stars for *Balaams* hire
Dissolve into the common dross!
(p. 486, ll.61–64)

In the first two lines he includes a characteristic reference from the prophecy of *Malachi*, and in this context of a plea that the whole nation shall be cleansed by the righteousness of God, he uses the story of Balaam, as recorded in the *Book of Numbers*. The prophet Balaam's unworthiness in agreeing to serve the Princes of Moab is immediately exposed by the righteous anger of God. Vaughan is declaring bluntly at the end of this poem that at a time of great national upheaval and stress, when many are tempted to join the popular movements of the day for the sake of expediency, all people are nonetheless under the Divine dispensation, and therefore subject to the prophetic judgement of God.

Vaughan returns briefly to the lesson of Old Testament history in 'Providence', another poem which bears traces of the tensions through which he was living in the Puritan period. In many ways 'Providence' is reminiscent of several lyrics in the first part of his work, especially 'Religion', in its considerable emphasis upon God's direct intervention in the affairs of his people, and his willingness to save them in their great distress:

> Sacred and secret hand!
> By whose assisting, swift command
> The Angel shewd that holy Well,
> Which freed poor *Hagar* from her fears,
> And turn'd to smiles the begging tears
> Of yong, distressed *Ishmael*.
>
> (p. 505, ll.1–6)

What interests Vaughan in this story is evidently the direct appearance of an angel which immediately transformed Hagar's situation. But there is a second point of great significance. He plainly regarded this mystical communion between God and his servants as the essence of the religious encounter:

> How in a mystick Cloud
> (Which doth thy strange sure mercies shroud)
> Doest thou convey man food and money
> Unseen by him, till they arrive
> Just at his mouth, that thankless hive
> Which kills thy Bees, and eats thy honey!
>
> (p. 505, ll.7–12)

Henry Vaughan is regarded by many critics as a mystical poet, and this is usually explained by his own nature and the way he sees the world. There will be a fuller discussion of this point in the final chapter, but it is at least worth making the point here that for him the term 'Mystick' is an exact description of the way God deals with people. His interpretation of religious experience is, as always, supported by a mass of Biblical evidence. His reading of the Bible, and especially the New Testament revealed to him incident after incident where the providence of God had alone sustained man, though that providence had been rewarded by great ingratitude.

'The Rain-bow', just four poems later, is also much concerned with the eternal providence of God. It has several interesting features.

In the first place, Vaughan has chosen a group of Old Testament patriarchs quite deliberately to symbolize the entire world after the flood. He has concentrated on one line in particular, the line of Shem, probably because Shem, often thought to be the eldest son of Noah, was considered to be the Father of the Shemitic people. Moreover, all the patriarchs mentioned after him were of the line of Shem. Terah is of course the father of Abraham, Nahor and Haran, and Lot was Haran's son. So there is a sense in these lines that God was giving his promise and his blessing not only to individuals but different generations of individuals after the great curse of the Flood, which was incurred by man's sin. And that same promise and blessing are open to every generation of mankind, and to us:

> Still yong and fine! but what is still in view
> We slight as old and soil'd, though fresh and new.
> How bright wert thou, when *Shems* admiring eye
> Thy burnisht, flaming *Arch* did first descry!
> When *Terah, Nahor, Haran, Abram, Lot*,
> The youthful worlds gray fathers in one knot,
> Did with intentive looks watch every hour
> For thy new light, and trembled at each shower!
>
> (p. 509, ll.1–8)

Secondly, Vaughan has attempted to give in his imagery

the feeling of the world as it was in the first books of the Bible, when all of experience was fresh and new. There is all the drama and majesty of the great descriptive passages of *Genesis* in the images of the 'burnish't, flaming Arch' and the 'youthful worlds gray fathers', and it is continued right through the poem in images of Nature in its most elemental forms. There is also a continual emphasis on the miracle of newness of life in God's creation:

> When thou dost shine darkness looks white and fair,
> Storms turn to Musick, clouds to smiles and air:
> Rain gently spends his honey-drops, and pours
> Balm on the cleft earth, milk on grass and flowers.
>
> (p. 509, ll.9–12)

Finally, as in so many of his poems which reflect the lives of Old Testament patriarchs and prophets, Vaughan pays great attention to the theme of the Fact of God in history. The sweep of historical event and the unfolding of God's purposes for man are handled with very great skill. The selection of his dramatic material is remarkable; so also is his ability to convey the narrative in bold terms without ever losing sight of his main theme, which is the fulfilment of God's promise to man, and man's neglect of it. The following passage shows with what ease he passes from the moral point to the illustration of it in epic terms, and then back to the moral point again:

> When I behold thee, though my light be dim,
> Distant and low, I can in thine see him,
> Who looks upon thee from his glorious throne
> And mindes the Covenant 'twixt *All* and *One*.
> O foul, deceitful men! my God doth keep
> His promise still, but we break ours and sleep.
> After the *Fall*, the first sin was in *Blood*,
> And *Drunkenness* quickly did succeed the flood;
> But since *Christ* dyed, (as if we did devise
> To lose him too, as well as *Paradise*,)
> These two grand sins we joyn and act together,
> Though blood & drunkeness make but foul, foul weather.
> *Water* (though both Heavens windows and the deep,
> Full forty days o'r the drown'd world did weep,)
> Could not reform us, and blood (in despight)

Yea Gods own blood we tread upon and slight.

(p. 510, ll.15–30)

Finally Vaughan leaves the great prophetic statement of God's presence in history and returns to the theme of the Judgement of God. The voice of the prophet calling the people back to God's righteousness becomes now a contemporary voice which none can escape:

For though some think, thou shin'st but to restrain
Bold storms, and simply dost attend on rain,
Yet I know well, and so our sins require,
Thou dost but Court cold rain, till *Rain* turns *Fire*.

(p. 510, ll.39–42)

'The Rain-bow' is one of the sharpest statements of judgement in his work. There is an important sense in which towards the end of the poem he takes upon himself the role of prophetic judge, and the fire which he prophesies, will consume the world unless his own generation turn from sin in time.

'The Stone', a few poems later in the collection, takes a central episode in Jewish history and builds upon it a further declaration of God's judgement. Vaughan's imagination was often fired by huge gatherings of the Jewish people and he pays particular attention to the words their great leaders gave to them. Here it is most important to know the text of his poem:

And Joshua said unto all the people, Behold, this stone shall be a witness unto us; for it hath heard all the words of the Lord which he spake unto us: it shall be therefore a witness unto you, lest ye deny your God.

(A. V., *Joshua*, Ch. 24, v.27)

Upon the tablets of stone were inscribed the words of the covenant between God and the people, that they would reject strange gods and serve only God, the Lord.

The most notable feature of the poetic sermon which Vaughan writes, is the opportunity which Joshua's words provide, to indulge in the theme so dear to him, that inanimate nature was better able to respond to the will of God, and to express the glory of the Creation. And this is one of the few occasions in his work where he actually claims to have come by this knowledge through a special insight:

> But I (Alas!)
> Was shown one day in a strange glass
> That busie commerce kept between
> God and his Creatures, though unseen.
>
> (p. 515, ll.18–21)

By direct intuitive experience, therefore, Vaughan is claiming to have knowledge of the essential procedures of God's judgement. God does not judge man by any method except that of His own Righteousness. Man is not condemned directly by God, but rather convicts himself, and knows, in justice, that he has sinned. It is a passage in which one feels he needs prose to make his message as detailed as he would have it be. He strains to make his meaning plain, but there is no doubt of the passion with which he holds his view:

> They hear, see, speak,
> And into loud discoveries break,
> As loud as blood. Not that God needs
> Intelligence, whose spirit feeds
> All things with life, before whose eyes,
> Hell and all hearts stark naked lyes.
> But he that judgeth as he hears,
> He that accuseth none, so steers
> His righteous course, that though he knows
> All that man doth, conceals or shows,
> Yet will not he by his own light
> (Though both all-seeing and all right,)
> Condemn men; but will try them by
> A process, which ev'n mans own eye
> Must needs acknowledge to be just.
>
> (p. 515, ll.22–36)

Vaughan is so steeped in the Bible and so much influenced by it that it is difficult to imagine that the only authority for his belief in the stones as active witnesses and recorders of man's behaviour is the episode from *Joshua*. Indeed the passage in which he works to his climax:

> Hence sand and dust
> Are shak'd for witnesses, and stones

> Which some think dead, shall all at once
> With one attesting voice detect
> Those secret sins we least suspect.
>
> (p. 515, ll.37–41)

bears very much the same sense as Christ's condemnation of the Pharisees on the Mount of Olives, when they asked Him to condemn the disciples for their acknowledgement of Him as Lord:

> And he answered and said unto them, I tell you that, if these should hold their peace, the stones would immediately cry out.
>
> (A. V., *Luke*, Ch. 19, v.40)

'The Stone' is not perhaps as clear or concise a statement as 'The Rain-bow' and its argument, for all its depth, is tortuous. But it continues, by other means, Vaughan's declaration of the judgement of God and when taken with 'The Rain-bow' it provides very convincing evidence that although he was anxious to emphasize the need for national reconciliation and peace in the poems towards the end of *Silex Scintillans* there is absolutely no watering down of the great prophetic message of God as Judge.

However, in 'Righteousness', which is placed near the end of his work, he seems to sum up the role and significance of the prophets in the most positive manner possible. There is no direct mention here of Judgement: instead he emphasizes the moral goodness of these men of God, who point the way by their example:

> Fair, solitary path! Whose blessed shades
> The old, white Prophets planted first and drest:
> Leaving for us (whose goodness quickly fades,)
> A shelter all the way, and bowers to rest.
>
> Who is the man that walks in thee? who loves
> Heav'ns secret solitude, those fair abodes
> Where turtles build, and carelesse sparrows move
> Without to morrows evils and future loads?
>
> (p. 524, ll.1–8)

'Righteousness' is certainly not free of the bitterness of the Civil War and its aftermath; Specific mention was made in the first chapter of the way in which Vaughan uses it to reveal his anguish. But that is not the principal note of the poem. Its central statement reflects clearly and exactly Vaughan's opening lines. The Prophets were those who declared the Righteousness of God, and he who is privileged to follow them upon what Vaughan frankly acknowledges to be a solitary path, is a man:

> Whose acts, words and pretence
> Have all one sense,
> One aim and end; who walks not by his sight:
> Whose eyes are both put out,
> And goes about
> Guided by faith, not by exterior light.
>
> (p. 525, ll.19–24)

It would be difficult to over-estimate the importance of Prophecy in the work of Henry Vaughan. It gave him the opportunity to use the whole of the Bible in the most direct and intimate manner. It reveals God in History and God in Judgement, and it sharpens and deepens his comment upon his own life and times. And finally it prepares the way for that central core of his work which declares above all the Revelation of a world changed and made new by the Spirit of God.

IV

'A DOOR OPENED IN HEAVEN'

In many of the poems studied so far it is clear that the influence of the *Book of Revelation* has been very considerable. 'Corruption', 'The Pilgrimage', 'The Constellation', 'The Seed growing secretly', and the elegy 'Thou that know'st for whom I mourne', to name but a very few, have depended both in thought and imagery upon the final book of the Bible and many other poems have relied upon the apocalyptic visions of some of the prophets, as was seen clearly in the previous chapter.

But there is a much larger group of poems, amongst them some of the best known lyrics he ever wrote, which are directly concerned with what Vaughan plainly sees as the unveiling of truth long hidden; dramatic pictures of future events, which display many of the qualities of apocalyptic literature. A number of these poems are based directly on texts from *Revelation*, and in one case from the *Book of Daniel* also. Many others, although based on texts or ideas in other parts of the Bible, share the same vision of life and the future of the world.

Nor is this any accident. There is no Preface to the first part of *Silex Scintillans*, so that the poems in that collection have to speak for themselves. But it is fair to assume that the Preface he wrote for the second part of his work, in 1654, was intended to be not only an explanation of the new poems, but to some extent a justification of the earlier ones too. There is no evidence to suppose that his broad aims were any different. And in this most important Preface, which might fairly be described as the key-note of his work, he specifically declares the aims of his work and marks the boundaries of his interest:

> 'It is true indeed, that to give up our thoughts to pious *Themes* and *Contemplations* (if it be done for pieties sake) is a great *step* towards perfection; because it will *refine*, and *dispose* to devotion and sanctity. And further, it will *procure* for us (so easily communicable is that *loving spirit*) some small *prelibation* of

those heavenly *refreshments*, which descend but seldom, and then very sparingly, upon *men* of an ordinary or indifferent *holyness;* but he that desires to excel in this kinde of *Hagiography*, or holy writing, must strive (by all means) for *perfection* and true *holyness*, that a *door may be opened to him in heaven*, Rev. 4.1. and then he will be able to write (with *Hierotheus* and holy *Herbert*) A true *Hymn.*'[1] (p. 392)

The verse from which he had quoted so conspicuously in the most substantial part of his Preface is the only occasion on which he makes a direct Biblical quotation in the whole of this quite lengthy and detailed exposition. It is important to examine the original passage in more detail. John is describing, in this fourth chapter, the throne of God, and he opens with these words:

'After this I looked, and, behold, a door was opened in heaven: and the first voice which I heard was as it were of a trumpet talking with me; which said, Come up hither, and I will show thee things which must be hereafter.

And immediately I was in the Spirit: and behold a throne was set in heaven and one sat on the throne.'

(A. V., *Revelation*, Ch. 4, v.1–2)

Although he refers, for the second time in the Preface, to George Herbert, Vaughan must have been well aware that the entire substance and style of his work was quite different from Herbert's.

His message, unlike Herbert, is immediately concerned with the declaration of a visionary truth, as was the writer of *Revelation*, and his style is much closer to the apocalyptic writers in its use of vivid colour and dramatic imagery. And there is another major difference. Vaughan, unlike Herbert, was writing in a period of great turmoil and upheaval, when religious persecution was widespread. He was, as we saw in the first section, directly concerned with the usurpation of the Church, and the attacks upon its adherents.

Immediately after his reference to *Revelation* Vaughan relates his aim directly to the work of the Church:

[1] Hierotheus was a character created by Dionysius, and introduced as his teacher in his work, *De Divinus Nominibus*. He was a supposed first century bishop of Athens who wrote inspiring hymns.

'To effect this in some measure, I have begged leave to communicate this my poor *Talent* to the *Church*, under the *protection* and *conduct* of her *glorious Head:* who (if he will vouchsafe to *own* it, and *go along* with it) can make it as useful now in the *publick*, as it hath been to me in *private*.'

(p. 392)

This is a fascinating passage. Christ was the Head of the Church Eternal, but as we have previously stated, the King was the Head of the Church temporal, and it is very difficult indeed to sustain the argument that Vaughan was not acknowledging the true ground of his poetry by emphasizing the entire context in which he wrote. The Church to which he belonged was in many places despoiled, and the earthly head of it was dead. Yet Vaughan emphasizes quite unashamedly his concern with both the Church and its leader in the justification for his work. It is a very thinly veiled declaration of his real allegiance and interest. Indeed, even his reference to Herbert may be intended to underline his political allegiance. George Herbert was an Anglican priest who represented the traditional values and fundamental principles of Anglicanism.

There is another deep connection between these two paragraphs of Vaughan's Preface, and the truths they seek to present. The fact is that Apocalyptic Literature has a long tradition of dissent, and in some cases open rebellion. This was true of both Jewish and early Christian traditions:

'Apocalyptic literature was always considered unorthodox by the leading Jews, though it suited the mood of an occupied country which detested its Roman overlords.' ... 'The history of Christian apocalyptic was similar. Revelation is thoroughly in the style of apocalyptic writing. From the Roman point of view it was seditious literature.'[1]

This, then, is the context and background of apocalyptic literature on which Vaughan relies so heavily. It was plainly the literature of underground resistance. And the actual substance of books such as *Daniel*, in the Old Testament, and *Revelation*, in the New, makes abundantly clear that the

[1] R. H. Preston and A. T. Hanson, The Torch Bible Commentaries, *The Revelation of Saint John the Divine*, S.C.M. Press, London, (1949), p. 16.

continual emphasis on the final coming together of all God's people when the world as we know it will be no more, is the very core of the message. The constant pleas for God's dramatic intervention in human history to stop the wickedness and corruption, and save his people from the misery of their present circumstances are not only spiritual statements, but have strong social and political content:

> 'Apocalypses were usually written at a time of crisis and danger. One of their purposes was to strengthen the believer at a time of persecution and to encourage him to stand firm.' ... 'Although apocalypses spring from profound faith and burning conviction, the writers generally despair of the present and pin all their hopes on the future. They look for some great divine intervention in the near future, often on a world-wide scale, to put an end to an intolerable situation.'[1]

It is perfectily true that there are many notes in *Silex Scintillans*, besides the note of Apocalypse, but it is undeniable that Vaughan was acutely aware of the dangers which the Puritans had brought to the Church, the State and the ordinary people of his own locality. Furthermore, he was in a state of great depression and persistently laments not only the deep personal loss of his own friends, but widespread persecutions of his time. And this depression covers both parts of his work. There is no evidence whatever that the depression really lifts until towards the end of the second part, when his emphasis changes to some extent to reconciliation and a more positive yearning for peace. It is therefore no accident that he finds that the Apocalyptic writers, especially Daniel and John, suit his mood, and that he shares in large measure their vision of the world, and is so deeply influenced by their dramatic style and particularly by their imagery.

To take just one example, which will become clear in the detailed analysis of many of the poems: Vaughan uses time and again the principal images of the *Book of Revelation*. John makes frequent use of such images as 'Crown', 'White stone', 'Throne' and 'The Lamb'. And there is more allusion

[1] The Cambridge Bible Commentary, *The Revelation of John*, (Commentary by T. F. Glasson), Cambridge University Press, (1965).

to 'Angels' in *Revelation* than in any other Book of the Bible, and dramatic pictures of Angels with their sickles. Vaughan is obviously excited by all this imagery; these same images occur again and again in his poems, especially in the climaxes of his verse, often towards the end of the poem. And exactly like John in *Revelation* he lays considerable stress on the Christian pilgrim who 'overcometh' all the obstacles and persecutions of the present time and receives at last the 'Crown', or will appear in 'the Lamb's Book of Life'.

There are three particular areas of his work which appear to have been so directly influenced by apocalyptic vision that it would be impossible to ignore them. The first is his most dramatic and moving treatment of Darkness and Light, and all the remarkable imagery associated with it. The second is his preoccupation with newness of life, or the World made new, very often by God's dramatic intervention. And the third area is his great concern with the harmony of all Creation. The new world, into which all true Christians shall be received, is a comprehensive experience which excludes none of the natural glories God has created; trees, rivers, stones, birds, animals, insects, all are part of this new creation.

There is, of course, a good deal of overlapping, but it is necessary to explore these three areas separately, in order to understand how they form part of revelation as a whole.

DARKNESS AND LIGHT

In the second poem of *Silex Scintillans*, 'Death', Vaughan explores immediately the links between death and darkness. He expresses the natural revulsion of the body to the impending darkness of death:

> 'A neast of nights, a gloomie sphere,
> Where shadowes thicken, and the Cloud
> Sits on the Suns brow all the yeare,
> And nothing moves without a shrowd;'
>
> (p. 399, xx, ll.11–14)

He equates the light with the continuance of the Sun, as earlier seventeenth century poets have done. But the fascinating central feature of the poem is that, using two verses from the *Book of Job* as his base, he strongly asserts the fact of

Christian resurrection. The darkness of death is broken finally and only very gradually, by the redemption afforded to us in Christ:

> 'Then shall wee meet to mixe again, and met,
> 'Tis last good-night, our Sunne shall never set.'
>
> (p. 400, ll.31–2)

Vaughan thus applies the concept of a Christian heaven and Eternity to a Biblical book where there is no promise of Salvation. The whole point about righteousness in the *Book of Job* is that one cultivates it for its own sake, in order to perfect one's own moral goodness; there is no reward, except recognition of one's own worthiness. Vaughan could have chosen any text from the Gospels or Epistles to illustrate that the light revealed by Christ finally overcomes the darkness. His point in choosing Job is to assert that even here in the '*Land of darknesse, as darknesse it selfe, and of the shadow of death*' (*Job*, ch. 10, v.21–22) the light of Christ finally shines, although its people died before the promise was given. It is, of course, a theme explored several times by Paul in his letters, as Vaughan would be perfectly well aware. This statement, at the beginning of *Silex Scintillans*, is therefore well within the Christian tradition of the New Testament epistles.

'Resurrection and Immortality' which immediately follows it, owes even more to the statement of Christian belief in the Epistles, and especially to *Hebrews*, from which Vaughan takes his text. In many ways it is a continuation of the previous poem, and certainly seems to have been written at the same time or shortly afterwards, and deliberately placed to gain maximum effect in argument. These poems were, after all, written to persuade others of the truth, as Vaughan made clear in his Preface, and the theological argument was not unimportant to him. It is clearly unwise to assume that the poems in *Silex Scintillans* follow each other in sequence of composition; but one thing seems fairly certain, that Vaughan carefully arranges poems in sequence of thought throughout the first part, and again in Part Two.

'Resurrection and Immortality' owes a good deal to the idea of the New Covenant, which is central to the argument of the tenth chapter of *Hebrews*, and it is interesting that his images of darkness and light occur in the context of his entire vision of the newness of life, as reflected in the Epistle. His 'renewing breath' (1.1) contrasting boldly with 'loosens death' (1.2), is his own particular gloss on the 'new, and living way' of *Hebrews*, and he illustrates it by an extraordinarily rich and imaginative picture of the silk-worm, emerging slowly from darkness to light. Here there is none of the intellectual argument of Donne, or the careful moral structures of Herbert. Vaughan is absolutely on his own ground as he describes one tiny manifestation of Creation's transformation from darkness to light:

> Some drowsie silk-worme creepe
> From that long sleepe
> And in weake, infant hummings chime, and knell
> About her silent Cell
> Untill at last full with the vitall Ray
> She wing'd away,
> And proud with life, and sence,
> Heav'ns rich Expence,
> Esteem'd (vaine things!) of two whole Elements
> As meane, and span-extents.
>
> (p. 400–401, ll.5–14)

The 'renewing breath' grows until the Creature can live completely on its own, sustained only by the life-giving power of the Creator and the fusion of the physical and spiritual contains within it the full promise of Heaven. But Vaughan then pursues an immediate contrast between the insect and man, and establishes a pattern which will become familiar in many of his poems of revelation:

> Shall I then thinke such providence will be
> Lesse friend to me?
> Or that he can endure to be unjust
> Who keeps his Covenant even with our dust.
>
> (p. 401, ll.15–18)

Vaughan uses for the first time in *Silex Scintillans* an image of sinful man which becomes more or less standard throughout the collection. 'Dust' is mere dross, the perpetual sign that man is nothing without God. It is, in fact, a clever combination of meanings. The Lord God 'formed man of the dust of the ground' (*Genesis*, Ch. 2, v. 7); but 'dust' signifies also the end of man ... 'dust thou art and unto dust shalt thou return' (*Genesis*, Ch. 3, v. 19). To this Vaughan adds his own gloss, that 'dust' is the sin in man, the inevitable corruption which would end in annihilation without the redeeming mercy of Christ in the New Covenant.

Vaughan exploits this image of dust and especially the second meaning – 'unto dust shalt thou return' – in the opening statement of the Soul's reply, and uses it with great skill in his expression of the journey from darkness to light which cancels the power of death:

> And how of death we make
> A meere mistake,
> For no thing can to *Nothing* fall, but still
> Incorporates by skill,
> And then returns, and from the wombe of things
> Such treasure brings
> As *Phenix*-like renew'th
> Both life, and youth;
>
> (p. 401, ll.23–30)

The very complex passage which follows is an attempt by Vaughan to make sense of the Christian doctrine of the resurrection of the body. It is remarkable for the certainty of spiritual assurance, and his conviction that the very suffering of the body prepares for the release of the soul. Despite the complexity of the argument the writing has a rare lyrical beauty, and his contrast between the 'rot' of darkness and death (l.44) and the redeeming 'light' of the blessed underlines the entire passage:

> Nor are those births which we
> Thus suffering see
> Destroy'd at all; But when times restles wave
> Their substance doth deprave
> And the more noble *Essence* finds his house
> Sickly, and loose,
> He, ever young, doth wing
> Unto that spring,
> And *source* of spirits, where he takes his lot
> Till time no more shall rot

His passive Cottage; which (though laid aside,)
Like some spruce Bride,
Shall one day rise, and cloath'd with shining light
All pure, and bright
Re-marry to the soule, for 'tis most plaine
Thou only fal'st to be refin'd againe.

(p. 401–402, ll.136–50)

The 'house' imagery is characteristic of the *Epistle to the Hebrews*. The 'house' becomes the dwelling place of the spirit. If the spirit is not in Christ then the house is 'Sickly, and loose'; but if Christ dwells in the man then his house is secure for ever:

> 'But Christ as a son over his own house; whose house are we, if we hold fast the confidence and the rejoicing of the hope firm unto the end.
>
> (A. V. *Hebrews*, Ch. 3, v.6)

The general sense of 'Bride' is the same as in the well-known vision of John (*Revelation*, Ch. 21) in which the holy city itself, the New Jerusalem, becomes a bride, as a signal that the day of the new world has now dawned. Furthermore, Vaughan has even copied the detail of the vision '... the bride, the Lamb's wife. .... Having the glory of God: and her light was like unto a stone most precious .....' (A. V. *Revelation*, Ch. 21, vv.9–11).

The third and final stanza of the poem is nothing less than a vision of Eternity, and the characteristics of the apocalyptic revelation are quite unmistakable in both thought and imagery. The very first line 'Then I that here saw darkly in a glasse' prepares us for the vision of the life to come, with its obvious rephrasing of Paul's words 'For now we see through a glass, darkly;' (A. V. I *Corinthians*, Ch. 13, v.12) but most of the revelation which follows owes a very great deal to the *Book of Daniel* and also the *Book of Revelation*. Vaughan acknowledges his debt to *Daniel* at the end of the poem. Certainly, his emphasis on light and on stars is very similar to Daniel's vision:

> 'And many of them that sleep in the dust of the earth shall awake, some to everlasting life, and some to shame and everlasting contempt.

> And they that be wise shall shine as the brightness of the firmament; and they that turn many to righteousness as the stars for ever and ever.'
>
> (A. V., *Daniel*, Ch. 12, vv.2–3)

Then, in the last few lines of the poem there is the clear note of *Revelation*:

> . . . . we shall there no more
> Watch stars, or pore
> Through melancholly clouds, and say
> *Would it were Day*!
> One everlasting *Saboth* there shall runne
> Without *Succession*, and without a *Sunne*.
>
> (p. 402, ll.65–70)

In this closing part of the vision there appears to be a translation, in general terms of John's famous vision of the New Jerusalem:

> 'And the city had no need of the sun, neither of the moon, to shine in it: for the glory of God did lighten it, and the Lamb is the light thereof.'
>
> (A. V. *Revelation*, Ch. 21, v.23)

'Resurrection and Immortality' is an important central statement of belief which links resurrection with direct revelation. It was impossible for Vaughan to conceive of re-birth without a vision of eternity, and this is so from the very commencement of his work in *Silex Scintillans*. The vision of Heaven is not something he works up to as he delves deeper into spiritual experience and writes more; it is something he starts with. Essentially all the ingredients of the more famous statements of revelation in the second part, 'Ascension-Hymn', 'They are all gone into the world of light!' and 'The Water-fall' are already here. And it is vital to realize that from the very beginning his vision is an intensely personal one, more personal than either Donne or Herbert. But at the same time the vision is more directly based upon Biblical sources than either of those poets. Vaughan reflects quite directly verses and whole passages from the apocalyptic books and from the Epistles, but he identifies himself so completely with their experiences that there is no unnecessary artifice or spoiling of effect. It is a rare achievement.

'The Lampe' is not centrally concerned with the journey from darkness to light, but rather with the importance of Christian preparedness. But the familiar text from Mark's gospel (*Mark*, Ch. 13, v.35) – 'for ye know not when the master of the house cometh, at even, or at midnight' is too good an opportunity for Vaughan to miss. It is obvious that the night fascinates him. But the interesting facet of this poem is the blend of grimness and beauty which characterizes his description of the hours of darkness; it half repels him and half attracts:

> 'Tis dead night round about: Horrour doth creepe
> And move on with the shades; stars nod, and sleepe,
> And through the dark aire spin a firie thread
> Such as doth gild the lazie glow-worms bed.
>
> (p. 410, ll.1–4)

Already he discerns the positive qualities of darkness, and later in *Silex Scintillans* his vision of darkness grows and changes; but here darkness is still partly equated with 'horrour'.

'The Incarnation, and Passion' has both depth and great beauty. Vaughan explores the conflict between darkness and light in the specific context of Christ's birth and death. Whereas in 'Resurrection and Immortality' he was concerned with his own individual progress from this world to Eternity, and gave no direct allusions to the person of Christ, he now uses Christ as a model, and the images of light and darkness are woven into the pattern of Christ's birth and death:

> To put on Clouds instead of light,
> And cloath the morning-starre with dust,
> Was a translation of such height
> As, but in thee, was ne'r exprest;
>
> (p. 415, ll.5–8)

Here again Vaughan reflects the imagery of different books of the Bible. The morning-star is, of course, one of his favourite images. It is used in different parts of the Bible, and especially in the *Book of Job* – 'the morning stars sang together, and all the sons of God shouted for joy'. (*Job*, Ch. 38, v.7). And in *Revelation* it is given a place of great honour. In the very final vision Christ describes himself as 'the root and the offspring of David, and the bright and morning star'. (*Revelation*, Ch. 22, v.16). Throughout this short poem it is the speed with which Vaughan contrasts light and darkness which is so striking.

In the third stanza he continues the very quick contrasts, and manages to make profound Biblical truth simple and intimate:

> Brave wormes, and Earth! that thus could have
> A God Enclos'd within your Cell,
> Your maker pent up in a grave,
> Life lockt in death, heav'n in a shell;
>
> (p. 415, ll.9–12)

He stresses the homeliness of the Resurrection; the passage from death to life, through darkness to light, is short and swift because Christ has made it possible.

In the fourth and fifth stanzas there is the same certainty and sense of triumph. One image suffices to describe the condition of unregenerate man – 'rebellious clay', which recalls several parts of the Bible, but especially the *Book of Job*. But there is no discussion of the power of Christ's redemption. It is enough to know that it is available, and cancels all the terror of death.

Two of the untitled elegies Vaughan wrote, almost certainly as laments for the death of William, are interesting in that they offer a sharp contrast in style and mood. 'Come, come, what doe I here?' must be one of the starkest and most poignant of all his elegies. There is great emphasis on the counting of hours and days and his view of time is of a long passage to be lived through until one is called out of time. There is no direct Biblical reference or allusion. Most significantly, there is no light at the end of the passage of time. The images of darkness in the final stanza – 'a tombe', 'a dark, and seal'd up wombe' have nothing of the ring of resurrection of earlier poems. And the last four lines of the elegy express no sure confidence, only longing to be reunited with the loved one.

> But I would be
> With him I weep
> A bed, and sleep

To wake in thee.

(p. 420, ll.27–30)

There is not a single mention of light, to counter the weight of darkness and despair.

'Silence, and stealth of days!' shares the same preoccupation with Time. It is, if anything, more intense because he has actually counted the hours; and there is the same brooding melancholy in the poem's opening:

Silence, and stealth of days! 'tis now
  Since thou art gone,
Twelve hundred houres, and not a brow
  But Clouds hang on.

(p. 425, ll.1–4)

But despite the initial heaviness, the mood breaks. The very next picture is of a 'solitary lamp' (l.7) and then he reverses time, and makes a 'retreat/Unto that hour/Which shew'd thee last,' (ll.13–15). And perhaps most important of all, though William's light was in the end extinguished, at least Vaughan remembers that there was 'light, and pow'r,' (l.16).

There is also a celebration of the brightness of Eternity, which was completely absent from the earlier elegy. There may well be darkness in death for many, and they shall sleep in the 'common urn' (l.22) but there is now an absolutely clear statement by Vaughan that those who sleep in darkness are separated from God's elect:

But those fled to their Makers throne,
  There shine, and burn;
O could I track them! but souls must
  Track one the other,
And now the spirit, not the dust
  Must be thy brother.

(p. 426, ll.23–28)

The 'one *Pearle*' (l.29) which leads him to the light may, as some critics have suggested, be his wife. But it is useless to speculate. A rather stronger argument could be made for the Bible itself, which gives him the truth. What is certain is that these two remarkably sensitive elegies taken together bring us from the depth of despair to a confident assertion of the light of the Blessed.

Placed just before this elegy is the short but very powerful lyric 'The Evening-watch', a dialogue between the Body and the Soul in which Vaughan explores the theme of darkness and light in the context of Time and Eternity. The 'sleep' in the first line, implying darkness and possibly death, is neatly counterbalanced by the familiar image of the 'day-star' with its connotation of the presence of Christ and the hope of awakening to a final Resurrection.

The reply of the soul emphasizes that the body in death will be 'Unnumber'd', and so carries the clear implication that man becomes merely part of God's 'dust'. Once again the 'dust' (l.7) is a clear reminder of the frailty of man's body and also the sin in man. But the grimness of 'Unnumber'd in thy dust' is beautifully contrasted with the great Christian hope, that each 'dust' is recorded, and that the promise of God in Christ shall be complete:

> Goe, sleep in peace; and when thou lyest
> Unnumber'd in thy dust, when all this frame
> Is but one dramme, and what thou now descriest
> In sev'rall parts shall want a name,
> Then may his peace be with thee, and each dust
> Writ in his book, who ne'r betray'd mans trust!
>
> (p. 425, ll.3–8)

The second question of the Body introduces the theme of mortal time contrasted with the timelessness of Eternity – 'How many hours do'st think 'till day?'. But the immediate reply of the Soul announces the utter impossibility of measuring Heaven by earthly standards:

> Heav'n
> Is a plain watch, and without figures winds
> All ages up;
>
> (p. 425, ll.11–12)

The last three lines of the poem have distinct traces of Platonism, especially of Socrates' illustration of the Philosopher and the Cave, in *The Republic*. 'Dayes, and hours are *Blinds*' is not only a reminder that man's whole concept of time is a delusion and a deception, but also implies that earthly life is lived in darkness. Only when one has completely thrown off the notion of time, may one begin to partake of Eternity:

....The last gasp of time
Is thy first breath, and mans *eternall Prime.*
(p. 435, ll.14–16)

The sharpness and clarity of 'The Evening-watch' rest squarely on its conciseness and the very sure technical mastery of such a complex subject. Those critics who have doubted Vaughan's technical ability and control of the emotional tone of his verse should note it well.

A more direct Christian statement of the significance of the Resurrection for each individual soul is contained in 'Buriall' in which Vaughan returns to the *Epistle to Romans* which obviously interested him very greatly. In both thought and image the poem is deeply Pauline, and its fascination is in the very skilful association of the images of disintegration and decay. In the first stanza Vaughan links death, sleep, and darkness with guilt. There is the clear implication that the state of darkness is the inevitable result of human sin; there is no recognition whatever that this darkness is a blessed state, although in the end, by the mercy of God, redemption is possible. There is, even in the darkness of 'senseless sleep' (1.4) some hope:

O then,
Thou great Preserver of all men!
Watch o're that loose
And empty house,
Which I sometimes liv'd in.
(p. 427, ll.6–10)

The imagery of the house which Vaughan has already used briefly in 'Resurrection and Immortality' is continued in the second stanza. It is in fact a very apt and clever adaptation of the Pauline doctrine of Christian fidelity. Every man builds a house, which is indeed the structure of his own mortal life:

'For every house is builded by some man; but he that built all things is God.

And Moses verily was faithful in all his house, as a servant, for a testimony of those things which were to be spoken after;'
(A. V. *Hebrews*, Ch. 3, vv.4–5)

And there are more general Pauline echoes in the language and thought of the third verse:

> And nothing can, I hourely see,
> Drive thee from me,
> Thou art the same, faithfull, and just
> In life, or Dust;
>
> (p. 428, ll.21–24)

This recalls the apostle's constant emphasis on the impossibility of anything separating him from the love of God, and also the theme of Christ's complete fidelity, however unfaithful the Christian might be – 'Jesus Christ the same yesterday, and to-day, and for ever'. (A. V. *Hebrews*, Ch. 13, v.8) The description of his own life as 'crumm'd' (l.25), recalls the 'Virgin-Crums' in another of his poems of Death – 'The Burial of an Infant' but the effect here is the opposite. His life is unfaithful and therefore broken into pieces; only the confidence that he is part of God's 'Clay' (l.30) which can be fashioned as God wills, is able to sustain him. In the final stanza he returns yet again to the subject of Time. He is saddened and frustrated by the 'delay' of time here and now, yet time is the servant of God and can bring him to God's eternity. In the poem's last line there is a plea for the most speedy delivery from the bondage of earthly time – 'O come Lord *Jesus* quickly!' (l.40).

'Disorder *and* frailty' is very interesting in the development of his thought. It represents vividly the elemental struggle between evil and goodness, darkness and light in his own soul and goes much further than his previous poems in equating darkness with the death of the spirit which has been caused by sin:

> When first thou didst even from the grave
> And womb of darknes becken out
> My brutish soul, and to thy slave
> Becam'st thy self, both guide, and Scout;
> Even from that hour
> Thou gotst my heart; And though here tost
> By winds, and bit with frost
> I pine, and shrink
> Breaking the link
> 'Twixt thee, and me; And oftimes creep

Into th' old silence, and dead sleep,
Quitting thy way
All the long day,
Yet, sure, my God! I love thee most.
Alas, thy love!

(pp. 444–5, ll.1–15)

The conflict is much sharper than in 'Regeneration', and the extremes of mood much greater. It is an extremely apt personal commentary on the famous sixth chapter from *Hosea* from which the text is taken, and Vaughan makes excellent use of the 'dew' in Hosea's original passage, transforming it, as in so many of his other poems, into the blood of Christ which alone can save him. But the intensity of the conflict far surpasses anything which is in the prophecy of *Hosea*. Vaughan's journey from darkness to light is short and swift, and his dramatic images have a touch of violence:

I threaten heaven, and from my Cell
Of Clay, and frailty break, and bud
Touch'd by thy fire, and breath;

(p. 445, ll.16–18)

All the images of man's frailty and God's power are ones Vaughan has used many times before – 'cell', 'clay', 'fire', 'breath', but in the last stanza the exaltation of his plea to be with God has a fierce passion and personal intensity which bears the true mark of apocalyptic writing:

...... but give wings to my fire,
And hatch my soul, untill it fly
Up where thou art, amongst thy tire
Of Stars, above infirmity;

(p. 446, ll.46–49)

Although there is no direct reference to Time in this lyric, the call for a release from mortal frailty and a sight of Paradise is immediate. As in *Daniel* and *Revelation*, the insistence is on urgent release and the experience of bliss now, not in some future time when the normal earthly span is run.

Probably the most developed exploration of darkness and light in the whole of Part One of *Silex Scintillans* is in 'The Dawning'. This is written entirely within the context of the revelation of God's glory; in the authentic style of the great apocalyptic books of the Bible its emphasis is almost completely on last things, the expectation of the coming of God. Vaughan announces his theme directly in the first four lines:

> Ah! what time wilt thou come? when shall that crie
> The *Bridegroom's Comming*! fil the sky?
> Shall it in the Evening run
> When our words and works are done?
>
> (p. 451, ll.1–4)

This is a clear reference to the familiar story in St. Matthew's gospel:

> 'While the bridegroom tarried, they all slumbered and slept.
> And at midnight there was a cry made, Behold, the bridegroom cometh; go ye out to meet him.
>
> (A. V. *Matthew*, Ch. 25, vv.5–6)

But the sleep of man is countered by the 'all-surprizing light' of God. (l.5). And the sleep is the sleep of darkness, the darkness of sin or triviality. The great beauty of Vaughan's writing lies in the intimacy and tenderness with which he characterizes the vision of God's coming:

> Or shal these early, fragrant hours
> Unlock thy bowres?
> And with their blush of light descry
> Thy locks crown'd with eternitie;
>
> (p. 452, ll.9–12)

The entire middle section of the poem is an expression of the total harmony of Nature, in which all aspects of the Universe play the parts ordained for them from the beginning of time. In this ideal picture darkness has no part. The darkness of night must be shed so that the full vision of God's glory may be revealed:

> The whole Creation shakes off night,
> And for thy shadow looks the light,
> Stars now vanish without number,
> Sleepie Planets set, and slumber,
> The pursie Clouds disband, and scatter,
> All expect some sudden matter,
> Not one beam triumphs, but from far

That morning-star;

(p. 452, ll.16–24)

The centrality of Christ is plainly recognized by Vaughan's use once again of the 'morning-star'. The only book of the New Testament which employs this image is the *Book of Revelation*, and as Vaughan's identification of the star with Christ is vital to his whole argument it is virtually certain that he takes it direct from the final chapter of *Revelation* which provides us with the most ecstatic vision of the coming of Christ:

> 'I Jesus have sent mine angel to testify unto you these things in the churches. I am the root and the offspring of David, and the bright and morning star.
>
> And the Spirit and the bride say, Come. And let him that heareth say, Come. . . . .'
>
> (A. V. *Revelation*, Ch. 22, vv.16–17)

The final section of 'The Dawning' is remarkable for two separate statements Vaughan makes. The first is the reminder that the coming of Christ will bring with it the judgement of 'poor careless man' (l.28). Vaughan rarely loses sight of the Judgement of God, just as he never forgets the message of deliverance from bondage which both the prophets and the gospels drive home. And these two aspects of God's work are always linked as Vaughan looks at the divided state of his country, and the condition of his own life. The political overtones are too obvious to need further emphasis. But the judgement here is far less frightening than in many of his other poems. There is nothing here of the sustained wrath in his second 'Day of Judgement' poem. The main emphasis, instead, is on the anticipation of joy in the kingdom of God.

This leads naturally to the second major statement, and the one which concludes the poem. Vaughan sees life with God as an experience of extraordinary liveliness and excitement. There are certainly a number of lyrics in *Silex Scintillans* in which he pleads only for peace and quiet security in the after-life, but not here. Indeed, his whole presentation of the struggle from darkness to light must be seen here within the framework of an active, purposeful eternity. His images of the darkness of sin – 'puddle' (l.29), 'Corrupt securitie' (l.30), 'dead' and 'grave' (l.31) are directly contrasted with images of the intense liveliness of Nature – 'restless, vocall *Spring*' (l.33) and 'run, and sing,' (l.34). He acknowledges that while here on earth he must still have some communication with the ordinary affairs of the world but designates them by a familiar image – the 'poor dust' (l.40) of darkness and inevitable death:

> And though (while here) of force I must
> Have Commerce sometimes with poor dust,
> And in my flesh, though vile, and low,
> As this doth in her Channel, flow,
> Yet let my Course, my aym, my Love,
> And chief acquaintance be above;
>
> (p. 452, ll.39–44)

But above all, it is the tremendous spiritual excitement, the anticipation of hope in the life everlasting which makes 'The Dawning' so individual an expression of faith. The mood of his closing lines matches exactly the final vision of *Revelation* to which reference has already been made. In both there is the absolute certainty that life with God will be the very beginning of real experience. Unlike the foolish virgins who were 'un-drest' expecting nothing, Vaughan declares he will be absolutely ready:

> So when that day, and hour shal come
> In which thy self wil be the Sun,
> Thou'lt find me drest and on my way,
> Watching the Break of thy great day.
>
> (p. 452, ll.45–48)

Concise, beautifully integrated in image and thought, and with a great clarity of vision, this is unquestionably one of Vaughan's finest poems; at one level extremely artful, at another level direct and simple, and very moving.

'The Holy Communion' is the last poem in the first part of *Silex Scintillans* which explores the theme of darkness and light, and it adds a new dimension to his work. Darkness is not inevitably linked with sin; it may often be a preparation for better things which the grace of God can bring. There is an interesting comparison between the soul's capacity to quicken the body through the sacred act of Communion with

Christ, and God's original creation of the world when 'the earth was without form, and void; and darkness was upon the face of the deep.' (A. V. *Genesis*, Ch. 1, v.2):

> Thus soules their bodies animate,
> And thus, at first, when things were rude,
> Dark, void, and Crude
> They, by thy Word, their beauty had, and date;
>
> (p. 457. ll.5–8)

This important idea that everything which lives, created by God, has an opportunity to be restored to full glory, is for the first time given real prominence in his work. And he develops the idea. Did not God create the darkness as well as the light? Are they not both manifestations of his character and purpose:

> All were by thee,
> And stil must be,
> Nothing that is, or lives,
> But hath his Quicknings, and reprieves
> As thy hand opes, or shuts;
> Healings, and Cuts,
> Darkness, and day-light, life and death
> Are but meer leaves turn'd by thy breath.
>
> (p. 457, ll.9–16)

It is a theme which he will pursue in greater detail in the second part of *Silex Scintillans*, and especially in 'The Night'.

Only life without God is real abiding darkness which never breaks. Vaughan characterizes this as 'blackness' (l.18) but immediately contrasts it with the necessary darkness which fell upon the world at the death of Christ. This is the darkness which prepares us for light, the state we have to pass through in order to see God. And this transformation from darkness to light is made for ever part of the Christian's experience through the sacrament of the blood of Christ. In this important passage Vaughan seems not only to accept but even to welcome the darkness:

> But that great darkness at thy death
> When the veyl broke with thy last breath,
> Did make us see
> The way to thee;
>
> *   *   *   *   *   *

Thou dost unto thy self betroth
  Our souls, and bodies both
  In everlasting light.

(p. 458. ll.21–24 and 30–33)

Although 'The Holy Communion' is not as powerful a poem as 'The Dawning' it has fine passages. And it also leads the way forward to the poems in the second part of *Silex Scintillans*, especially the positive view of darkness as expressing something essential about the nature of God and the World He created.

In the second part there are very few poems which explore the revealed world primarily in terms of darkness and light. There are lyrics in the collection which employ images of darkness and light as a general background to other subjects, and in some of these Vaughan still presents the spiritual conflicts of his own life in terms of the endless battle between the darkness of sin and the light of God's truth. But such lyrics are far less frequent than they were in the first part. If one takes, for example, a very important poem like 'The Proffer', the fifth poem in Part Two, one can see immediately that there is a great tension expressed in it. Vaughan's mood in the poem is anguished, and there were very powerful political and social reasons for his anguish.[1] He is also aware of the deep, spiritual conflicts in himself. Yet none of these tensions or conflicts are expressed by any of the images of darkness which we have just found in so many poems in Part One.

There are, however, three lyrics which make important statements about the nature of darkness and the night, and develop the theme of the way in which darkness prepares us for light, which we have already noted in 'The Holy Communion'.

The first of these lyrics, 'Jesus weeping' (second poem), is based directly on the words 'Jesus wept' from John's Gospel. (A. V. *John*, Ch. 11, v.35). The poem as a whole is a protracted lament on the subject of death. Its great beauty lies in Vaughan's ability to convey the tenderness of Christ, so that

[1] See Chapter 1, pp. 41–43.

even his tears become a blessing, enabling the dead to live again after the final resurrection. It is an intimate and moving picture:

> O holy groans! Groans of the Dove!
> O healing tears! the tears of love!
> Dew of the dead! which makes dust move
> And spring, how is't that you so sadly grieve,
> Who can relieve?
>
> (p. 504, ll.9–13)

The great Biblical symbols of 'Dove' and 'Dew' have been discussed in detail already. 'Dove' symbolizes the spirit of the Lord, and 'dew' is the refreshment of God's spirit which has renewed man ever since the days when the Israelites wandered in the desert. Now it makes the 'dust move'.

The middle section of the poem treats death confidently. This is no mournful dirge for those who have died but a complete conviction that 'thou canst restore/All better far then 'twas before;' (p. 504. ll.36–37). It is remarkable that there is no doubt or anguish in this poem. Sin may be constant but it is never directly mentioned here.

The same note of confidence is seen in the final section of the poem. Although Vaughan says his 'business here shall be to grieve' (l.45), this is clearly the necessary and natural grief of the penitent Christian soul. It is a grief which obviously leads to joy, and the endurance of a temporary darkness that will be made light:

> A grief that shall outshine all joys
> For mirth and life, yet without noise.
> A grief, whose silent dew shall breed
> Lilies and Myrrhe, where the curs'd seed
> Did sometimes rule. A grief so bright
> 'Twill make the Land of darkness light;
> And while too many sadly roam,
> Shall send me (*Swan-like*) singing home.
>
> (p. 505, ll.46–53)

Vaughan selects one of the most exotic images from the *Song of Solomon* to symbolize the love that springs from his grief. It provides a beautiful contrast between the idealization of his love and the symbol of man's degeneration. But 'curs'd seed' is an interesting image. It certainly conveys the original fall of man from grace, but is probably also a reference to the oppressions of his own day, and this reading would seem to be confirmed by his pointed use of 'Land of darkness' in the next line. Whatever the darkness, whatever the grief, the promise of man's redemption is sufficient cause for complete satisfaction and joy.

In 'The Holy Communion' Vaughan's view that darkness prepares us for light was brief and exploratory. But in 'Jesus weeping' there is an acceptance and a serenity of mood which can take suffering and grief in its stride. This enables him to assert with complete assurance that light can shine in darkness. There is no terror even in the darkness of death because it is merely a phase before the final resurrection.

The other two poems which make substantial statements on the subject of Darkness and Light are both in the last two dozen poems of *Silex Scintillans*. They are 'As time one day by me did pass' and 'The Night'; both are deeply impressive pieces of work.

'As time one day' is an untitled elegy. It is impossible to determine with any certainty the exact subject of his lament. It might once again be for his brother William, who has inspired at least two of the very distinguished elegies in *Silex Scintillans*. On the other hand it could easily be for Catherine, who had certainly died before the completion of the second part of *Silex Scintillans*. Hutchinson's view that 'Fair and yong light!' probably 'commemorates the death of his wife Catherine, while he was engaged in writing the second part of *Silex Scintillans*' seems sound enough although there is obviously no conclusive evidence for it.[1] If one accepts the view, then it may well be that in 'As time one day', which is placed immediately before it in the collection, there are also references to Catherine. But a number of Vaughan's close friends who had suffered under the Puritan regime had died since he first started writing *Silex Scintillans*, and it could be for any one of them.

What cannot be in any doubt is the general influence of the *Book of Revelation* upon his style and thought in this

[1] See Hutchinson, op. cit., p. 107.

poem. It is a two-fold influence. Firstly, the directness of the vision, emphasized by Vaughan's immediate and urgent treatment of it in the first stanza, has much of the personal authenticity and boldness of approach used in *Revelation*, especially in the fourth chapter from which he has already directly quoted in his Preface:

> 'After this I looked, and, behold, a door was opened in heaven: and the first voice which I heard was as it were of a trumpet talking with me; which said, Come up hither, and I will show thee things which must be hereafter.'
>
> (A. V. *Revelation*, Ch. 4, v.1)

Secondly, it is a vision of time and Eternity; in fact earthly time is suspended, and exactly as in *Revelation*, past and future time are mixed together. The record of 'past days' (l.5) leads inevitably to future events, although of course modes of time become meaningless in the end because, as in many apocalyptic writings, the whole of Creation is being seen under an aspect of Eternity. The principal images of Vaughan's vision are also deeply influenced by some of the main visionary glimpses of the New Testament. The 'dusky glasse' of time (l.2) is very similar to 'through a glass, darkly' of *I. Corinthians* (Ch. 13, v.12), and the 'book' of time recalls the many references to the 'book of life' in *Revelation*. In the book the 'ev'n, smooth lines, like the Suns rays' (l.11) recalls the great vision of Isaiah, echoed by Luke, that 'the rough ways shall be made smooth'. (A. V. *Luke*, Ch. 3, v.5).

In the third stanza the reference to youth sugests that the lament is certainly for a young friend, but that could include both Catherine and William. The greatness of Vaughan's writing is the way he transforms the lament into a celebration:

> O bright and happy Kalendar!
> Where youth shines like a star
> All pearl'd with tears, and may
> Teach age, *The Holy way*;
> Where through thick pangs, high agonies
> Faith into life breaks, and death dies.
>
> (p. 512, ll.13–18)

The picture of youth teaching age is reminiscent of the final passage of 'Isaac's Marriage', in which Isaac is seen as a

Patriarch while still young, and also the most moving passage in 'An Epitaph upon the Lady *Elizabeth*' in which King Charles' second daughter is tested, while still very young, by all the afflictions normally experienced only in age. (p. 63, ll.15–22). Indeed the 'thick pangs, high agonies' may well recall the agonies of the Civil War itself and the pangs of death which were experienced by so many who themselves believed in 'The holy way'. This is certainly a passage in which the celebration of eternal joy springs quite directly from Vaughan's recollection of the sheer horror of the recent past; the political strains are very near the surface.

The life of the blessed comprehends night. There is now no attempt by Vaughan to outlaw the night as being a time of darkness. Even the 'grave' is 'Set with green herbs, glad hopes and brave.' (ll.23–24) and the very 'dust' which he has castigated in so many earlier poems as epitomizing sin and suggesting darkness, 'By hiding doth preserve'. (l.28). The darkness of death, which he has so often shunned in the first part of *Silex Scintillans*, is now seen as an integral part of Life Eternal:

> O calm and sacred bed where lies
> In deaths dark mysteries
> A beauty far more bright
> Then the noons cloudless light
> For whose dry dust green branches bud
> And robes are bleach'd in the *Lambs* blood.
>
> (p. 512, ll.31–36)

Once again Vaughan goes straight to the *Book of Revelation* to provide the very heart of his vision, and his selection of material is superb. He has been describing the agony of loss endured because of the horror of his own time, and he deliberately uses images which John originally employed when he was speaking of those who had suffered great persecution:

> 'And I said unto him, Sir, thou knowest. And he said to me, These are they which came out of great tribulation, and have washed their robes, and made them white in the blood of the Lamb.'
>
> (A. V. *Revelation*, Ch. 7, v.14)

This is an excellent example of Vaughan's use of Biblical

apocalypse. From the deep divisions and persecutions of his own period he turns to the direct vision of Eternity in which John describes a society without division or class, professing only the name of the Lamb. And even John's 'neither shall the sun light on them, nor any heat' (Ch. 7, v.16) is suggested by Vaughan's 'A beauty far more bright/Then the noons cloudless light'.

In the final stanza the only contrast between darkness and light is that between his own self – 'soul-lesse shadow' (l.41) – and the light of the blessed which he has already described. And as in the classics of apocalyptic literature, his fervent prayer is for release as soon as possible from the burdens of the present time, although he recognizes that for the moment, at least, no release is likely:

> Sleep happy ashes! (blessed sleep!)
> While haplesse I still weep;
> Weep that I have out-liv'd
> My life, and unreliev'd
> Must (soul-lesse shadow!) so live on,
> Though life be dead, and my joys gone.
> (p. 513, ll.37–42)

The most complete summary of Vaughan's view of Darkness and Light in the final part of *Silex Scintillans* is to be found in 'The Night' which is placed only eighteen poems from the end of his work. It is deservedly a very famous poem, and may well be directly influenced by the hermetic belief in the unique spiritual powers of the darkness of night.[1] But it is first and foremost a deeply Christian statement which must be taken directly in the context of his great and sustained interest in this theme throughout the whole of *Silex Scintillans*.

The poem opens with a most powerful image of the holiness and purity of God; followed by a series of images contrasting darkness and light:

> Through that pure *Virgin-shrine*,
> That sacred vail drawn o'r thy glorious noon
> That men might look and live as Glo-worms shine,
> And face the Moon:
> Wise *Nicodemus* saw such light

[1] See also pp. 183–187.

As made him know his God by night.

(p. 522, ll.1–6)

From the very first line Vaughan is deeply concerned with the intimacy of Christ's meeting with Nicodemus. The '*Virgin-shrine*' is a place set apart in its sacredness. Vaughan manages to convey far more than the idea of the virgin birth by which Christ came to the world. In 'virgin' he chooses one of the most powerful and emotive of all Biblical symbols. Time and again in Biblical literature virgin denoted a people, a city, or a whole nation set apart – the virgin, the daughter of Babylon, the daughter of Israel. In the New Testament especially the virgin is synonymous with that person who adheres steadfastly to Christ and rejects anything that would violate complete faithfulness to him. This is exactly the sense in which John uses it in *Revelation*, when he speaks of 'the hundred and forty and four thousand which were redeemed from the earth':

> 'These are they which were not defiled with women; for they are virgins. These are they which follow the Lamb whithersoever he goeth. These were redeemed from among men, being the first-fruits unto God and to the Lamb.'
>
> (A. V. *Revelation*, Ch. 14, v.4)

This most powerful image of the purity of God's elect is then combined with an image of sacredness, to denote the marvel and wonder of this particular night meeting. Vaughan deliberately selects the 'vail' because it is a symbol of holiness. In the time of Moses the veil of blue, and purple and scarlet, divided the holy of holies which represented the highest heaven, from the holy place where the Church militant, or its representatives, met and served God. Such is the use of the veil in the *Book of Exodus*. But the veil, in the symbolism of the New Testament, had assumed an even greater importance. It typified the human nature of Christ, adorned with excellent gifts and graces, by which he had opened the way to Heaven for all his true believers:

> 'Having therefore, brethren, boldness to enter into the holiest by the blood of Jesus.
>
> By a new and living way, which he hath consecrated for us, through the veil, that is to say, his flesh;'
>
> (A. V. *Hebrews*, Ch. 10, vv.19–20)

The night therefore becomes the place of the presence of Christ, and the sacredness of the veil is emphasized even further by the dramatic rending of the veil of the temple when Christ was crucified; the separation of Jew and Gentile, and indeed all separation of men from one another is removed by the reconciliation which Christ achieved. The rending of the veil may well be termed the consummation of Christ's life in this respect.

But the picture of the glow-worms, so typical of Vaughan, brings to the high and splendid Biblical symbolism a touch of intimacy, and a reminder of the delight Vaughan took in all of Nature and in its innate capacity to respond to its Creator. This extremely rich and complex picture of the holiness and positive power of darkness is arguably the most concentrated and developed series of images he ever achieved in the opening stanza of any of his religious poems.

In the second stanza Vaughan develops his view of the true blessedness of darkness:

> Most blest believer he!
> Who in that land of darkness and blinde eyes
> Thy long expected healing wings could see,
> When thou didst rise,
> And what can never more be done,
> Did at mid-night speak with the Sun!
>
> (p. 522, ll.7–12)

The entire stanza is built upon the promise that Jesus would come to redeem not only Israel but the world. In Biblical terms 'he that will come' is a synonym for 'the expected one'. The 'long expected Jesus' is historically the fulfilment of the great prophetic visions of the Old Testament, and Vaughan with his tremendous knowledge of the Bible is exactly reflecting the persistent question asked of Jesus in the early days of his preaching and faithfully recorded in the Gospels, and especially Matthew:

> '..... Art thou he that should come, or do we look for another?'
>
> (A. V. *Matthew*, Ch. 11, v.3)

So, from the early poems of *Silex Scintillans*, in which darkness is almost always portrayed as the result of sin and spiritual neglect, Vaughan has progressed to the point where to see the promised Jesus, and to realize his full power and glory, it is necessary to accept the darkness. Far from impeding vision, it actually makes possible a full and intimate view of the Son of God, and 'Sun' (light) of the world.

As if to point the great importance of his discovery that darkness does not lead to inevitable death Vaughan achieves in the third and fourth stanzas the most remarkable and subtle contrasts between the darkness of death and darkness as a prelude to eternity. So the 'dead and silent hour' (l.14) enhances the 'hallow'd solitary ground' (l.15) and prepares for all the 'fulness of the Deity' (l.18). And the 'dead and dusty *Cherub*' and 'carv'd stone' (l.20) with their immediate associations with Church architecture are contrasted with Christ's 'living works'. The darkness and deadness of the stones by which men have sought to commemorate and worship Him are entirely eclipsed by the living Universe which constantly praises God:

> Where *trees* and *herbs* did watch and peep
> And wonder, while the *Jews* did sleep.
>
> (p. 522, ll.23–24)

It is the sheer intimacy of the picture which seizes and holds the imagination, but the development of it in one single line shows a masterly compression of Biblical truth. The sleeping of the Jews conveys far more than the background to the night conversation of Christ and Nicodemus. It includes a condemnation of those who slept, while Christ prayed for His Life; this happened on several occasions during His Ministry, and most notably in the Garden of Gethsemane. Vaughan's clear reference to '*Christs* progress, and his prayer time' in the fifth stanza (l.29) shows how influenced he was by the sacred ritual of Christ's life and especially the deliberate preparation for his sacrificial death:

> '.... and at night he went out, and abode in the mount that is called the mount of Olives.'
>
> (A. V. *Luke*, Ch. 21, v.37)

The strength and quality of Vaughan's vision in 'The Night' lies in the quite extraordinary way he has combined the depth of his feeling for a natural world which can so spontaneously and joyfully respond to the touch of the Creator, with his absolute belief in the dedication and discipline of Christ's life in which there is nothing accidental at all. It is the preordained will of God to redeem the world, and the 'progress' of Christ completely reveals it.

The fifth stanza also extends his view of darkness as an instrument of God's will:

> Dear night! this worlds defeat;
> The stop to busie fools; cares check and curb;
> The day of Spirits; my souls calm retreat
> Which none disturb!
>
> (p. 522, ll.25–28)

The contrast between the restlessness of the world and the calm sublimity of the night has never been clearer in all his poetry, and the cumulative effect of many short images heightens the emotional intensity. The picture of Christ is probably the warmest and most intimate he has ever achieved. Gone for the moment at least is the wrath of God, the righteous judge; in its place is a direct and strikingly fresh picture of Jesus, appearing in pastures of dew, which Vaughan has seen with his own eyes:

> Gods silent, searching flight:
> When my Lords head is fill'd with dew, and all
> His locks are wet with the clear drops of night;
> His still, soft call;
> His knocking time; The souls dumb watch,
> When Spirits their fair kinred catch.
>
> (p. 522, ll.31–36)

But Vaughan still sees himself as under the prophetic judgement of God. In the last three stanzas of the poem his plea for calm of spirit and union with God evokes some of the same images as he has used in 'Religion' in the first part of *Silex Scintillans.* The image of the tent and the request for the presence of angels recalls the great lyrical passages of Old Testament Prophecy in which angels appeared to the chosen ones of God. And as in 'Religion' he pleads for a special vision, a revelation of the direct glory of Eternity:

> Were all my loud, evil days

Calm and unhaunted as is thy dark Tent,
Whose peace but by some *Angels* wing or voice
Is seldom rent;
Then I in Heaven all the long year
Would keep, and never wander here.

(p. 523, ll.37–42)

The one great difference between the picture he presents here and that in 'Religion' is the plea for darkness. He returns again and again in 'The Night' to the theme of 'this worlds ill-guiding light' (l.47) and there is in the conclusion of this lyric a great deal of the world-weariness, frustration and pain which so obsesses him in the very next poem in the collection, 'Abels blood', in which he expresses his absolute horror at the shedding of blood. But for all this, there is no need to read into the last stanza of the poem mystic yearnings which are not necessarily intended:

There is in God (some say)
A deep, but dazling darkness; As men here
Say it is late and dusky, because they
See not all clear;
O for that night! where I in him
Might live invisible and dim.

(p. 523, ll.49–54)

Vaughan is certainly not the first Christian to have expressed a longing to live 'invisible' and even 'dim' in God's keeping. At one level it is no more than the penitence and humility of the Christian soul recognizing its limitations. One must read the verse in the context of the entire poem. 'The Night' is quite firmly based upon traditional Christian piety and Biblical thought and allusion, as even a brief analysis of its imagery shows. The plea for darkness in the final stanza is no stronger than his desire for 'deaths dark mysteries' and the 'beauty far more bright/Then the noons cloudless light' in 'As time one day by me did pass' (p. 512, ll.32–33). There is no new statement here. But there is in both these poems a recognition that darkness and light are relative terms, that God created all things, and that above all both darkness and light, as men perceive them and inadequately try to express them, are facets of the one unchanging face of God. And for this truth he had to look no further than the famous passage in the *Book of Psalms* which expresses it exactly:

> 'If I say, Surely the darkness shall cover me; even the night shall be light about me.
>
> Yea, the darkness hideth not from thee: but the night shineth as the day: the darkness and the light are both alike to thee.'
>
> (A. V. *Psalm* 139, vv.11–12)

But 'The Night' is a quite exceptional poem, exceptional in the clarity of its vision, in the fullness of its statement and above all in the spontaneity and inventiveness of its imagery. It is a complete experience, and there are few short lyrics in the canon of English religious poetry which surpass it.

THE WORLD MADE NEW

One of the most important and persistent ideas of apocalyptic writing, of all ages, is the desire for newness of life. There is often an overwhelming sense of frustration at the wickedness, perversity and cruelty of the world as experienced here and now on earth. And the *Book of Revelation* is certainly no exception. Throughout the work there is the constant yearning for a new, fresh, clean experience, the old rotten order swept away. Commentators on the apocalyptic writers have long recognized the urgency of this plea:

> 'We can understand how John, in company with the later Jewish apocalyptists and his fellow-Christians of the first century felt that the old earth, drooping under the weight of its crimes, scarred by countless insurrections of the still active powers of Chaos, was a place totally unfit for the final establishment of God's reign. The earth must pass; this is clear.'[1]

In *Revelation* the intensity of this feeling bursts into the dramatic declamation at the beginning of the twenty-first chapter:

> 'And I saw a new heaven and a new earth: for the first heaven and the first earth were passed away ....'
>
> (A. V. *Revelation*, Ch. 21, v.1)

[1] M. Kiddle, The Moffat New Testament Commentary, *The Revelation of St. John*, Hodder and Stoughton, London, (1940).

But a close study of this idea in apocalyptic writing shows plainly that the writers did not seek nor expect the complete destruction of the Universe, but rather its complete cleansing. What they wanted was renewal and restoration so that it would appear a new creation.

This is exactly the note sounded by Vaughan. Apart from a very few poems which recall the prophecies that the whole universe will be destroyed by fire, his vision depends upon the world made new, so that all that is corrupt, tired, and stale shall be completely done away by the restoration. And this longing for newness of life is in both parts of his work, although it is certainly more pronounced in the second part. It may well be that his extreme weariness with the violence and hatred of the Civil War and its aftermath, which we have already explored, intensified his natural spiritual inclination for a new Creation.

In the first part of *Silex Scintillans*, however, there are several important poems which, in both imagery and thought, concern themselves directly with the world made new. The first of these is 'Son-Dayes' in which Vaughan uses to the full a technique which he may have learned from the Welsh poets he had read in his youth. The technique is known in Welsh as *dyfalu*, and is mentioned briefly by Hutchinson in his short account of possible Welsh influences.[1] It consists of describing the subject by means of a large number of comparisons, usually in short phrases, so as to create a large cumulative effect because all the phrases very closely match one another. Vaughan writes the entire poem without using a single sentence, allowing his short descriptive phrases to do all the work:

> Bright shadows of true Rest! some shoots of blisse,
>   Heaven once a week;
> The next worlds gladnes prepossest in this;
>   A day to seek
>
> Eternity in time; the steps by which
> We Climb above all ages; Lamps that light
> Man through his heap of dark days; and the rich,

[1] See Hutchinson, op. cit., pp. 163–4.

And full redemption of the whole weeks flight.

(p. 447, ll.1–9)

Vaughan may also have been directly influenced in this by George Herbert, whose life and work he had quite unashamedly taken as a model for his own. Herbert does not use the technique very much but there is one notable example of it, 'Prayer' which Vaughan seems to have used as a starting-point; his own poem is in many respects very similar:

Prayer, the Churches banquet, Angels age,
  Gods breath in man returning to his birth,
The soul in paraphrase, heart in pilgrimage,
  The Christian plummet sounding heav'n and earth;

Several phrases in the Herbert poem have been echoed in Vaughan's poem. Despite the difference in subject matter Herbert's 'six-daies world' is recalled by Vaughan's 'six-days-showres' and the earlier poet's striking phrase 'Heaven in ordinarie' is rendered by the plainer 'Heaven here'.

But Vaughan's use of the technique of *dyfalu* is much more developed than Herbert's, and he deliberately employs the rapid accumulated images to raise the emotional tone of the poem to a high pitch. The main theme of the poem is that our life here is inextricably linked to Eternity. All through our lives we see flashes of Eternity and can recognize something of its radiance. God's sacred day affords all Christian believers an opportunity to glimpse Heaven here and now:

The Pulleys unto headlong man; times bower;
                    The narrow way;
Transplanted Paradise; Gods walking houre;
                    The Cool o'th' day;

The Creatures *Jubile*; Gods parle with dust;
Heaven here; Man on those hills of Myrrh, and flowres;
Angels descending; the Returns of Trust;
A Gleam of glory, after six-days-showres.

(p. 447, ll.9–16)

There is here quite direct evidence, if any were needed, that Vaughan is certainly not expressing a state of mystic otherness, a state of being completely removed from this life. The whole of the poem is firmly rooted in a well established mode of Christian piety, and the message is clear. God is accessible now; he has deliberately constructed a bridge to man. Once again Vaughan has used familiar Biblical stories and truths to make his points clear. Although the text from Matthew – 'narrow is the way, which leadeth unto life' (A. V. Ch. 7, v.14) is the most familiar, it is virtually certain that the visitation of the angel of God in the story of Balaam's Ass is the source of 'The narrow way' (1.10). He was very fond of this Old Testament narrative and as we have seen had made good use of it in other poems:

> 'And the angel of the Lord went further, and stood in a narrow place, where was no way to turn either to the right hand or to the left.'
>
> (A. V., *Numbers*, Ch. 22, v.26)

Indeed, the entire second stanza is dominated by the idea of God's direct intervention in the affairs of men, often through the agency of angels. 'Gods walking houre' and 'The Cool o'th' day' are open references to God's walking in the garden, from the *Genesis* story of Adam and Eve.

The complete picture shown us in the second stanza is of the world refashioned by the grace of God, and His direct intervention in the affairs of men. No single line sums it up better than 'Man on those hills of Myrrh, and flowres'. Vaughan has used *The Song of Solomon* several times in *Silex Scintillans* to denote the ideal reality, the world of full grace and perfect relationship with God. As in 'The Brittish Church' he slightly changes the wording; he also adds his own 'flowres' to the original Biblical phrase:

> 'Until the day break, and the shadows flee away, I will get me to the mountain of myrrh, and to the hill of frankincense.'
>
> (A. V., *The Song of Solomon*, Ch. 4, v.6)

In the final stanza, although there appears to be no direct Biblical reference or quotation, he even more confidently asserts the supremacy of the new life and the world restored:

> The Churches love-feasts; Times Prerogative,
> And Interest

Deducted from the whole; The Combs, and hive.
And home of rest.
(p. 447, ll.17–21)

The references to time are illuminating. In the first stanza – 'A day to seek/Eternity in time' (ll.4–5) suggests that time is suspended, while the experience of the world is still present. This is no leap into a future world without any concept of time; 'times bower' in the second stanza (l.9) reinforces the impression of all things suspended in time, and in the final stanza he goes further. Time on this one day becomes a measure of eternity for a brief span, both taking something away from time on earth and yet adding to the total quality of experience.

In the final four lines of the poem Vaughan stops only a little way short of Eternity itself. The way from Earth to Heaven is a blaze of light, a myriad stars and many suns, and the 'feast' of the last line is once again characteristic of *Revelation*, with its famous reference to 'the marriage supper of the Lamb' (A. V., *Revelation*, Ch. 19, v.9) upon which he later based his poem 'The Feast'.

The milky way Chalkt out with Suns; a Clue
That guides through erring hours; and in full story
A taste of Heav'n on earth; the pledge, and Cue
Of a full feast; And the Out Courts of glory.
(p. 448, ll.21–24)

There are two further poems towards the end of the first part of *Silex Scintillans* which are concerned with the extreme transitoriness of experience here on earth and a longing for the new Creation. They are 'The Pilgrimage' and 'The World'. We have already explored 'The Pilgrimage' as an important part of Vaughan's use of Prophecy. But as it occurs only two poems before 'The World', and seems in some respects to be a prelude to it, there are two additional aspects of the poem which should be made clear.

The first is that, recognizing he is a pilgrim travelling from earth to heaven, he emphasizes that he is in no sense a permanent part of the world's experiences. He considers himself to be merely waiting for the new spiritual reality to emerge. A great deal of the frustration of his present life breaks out in the lines:

So for this night I linger here,
And full of tossings too and fro,
Expect stil when thou wilt appear
That I may get me up, and go.

(p. 464, ll.9–12)

The second prominent note of 'The Pilgrimage' is his conviction that in his earthly experience he is now robbed of spiritual sight. And the pleading for this inner light by which he can comprehend the new creation contrasts directly with the 'night' (l.9) of the previous stanza:

I long, and grone, and grieve for thee,
For thee my words, my tears do gush,
O that I were but where I see!
Is all the note within my Bush.

(p. 464, ll.13–16)

'The World', with its celebrated vision of Eternity, is in very full measure an answer to the longing he has expressed in 'The Pilgrimage'. Much of the poem is of course preoccupied with the triviality of men here on earth, and we have already examined the political significance of the second stanza in some detail.[1] But there are a number of very striking features of his vision of Eternity.

The first is that although the poem takes as its starting point two verses in the *Epistle of John*, this is one of the few visionary poems he wrote in which there are almost no direct Biblical allusions. Until the last eight lines there is no mention of God or Christ, and little specific Christian theology. And yet the directness and boldness of his claim that he has seen Eternity has never been stronger in any of his poetry:

I saw Eternity the other night
Like a great *Ring* of pure and endless light,
All calm, as it was bright,
And round beneath it, Time in hours, days, years
Driv'n by the spheres
Like a vast shadow mov'd, In which the world

[1] See p. 30–31.

And all her train were hurl'd;

(p. 466, ll.1–7)

The only other two poems in his work which view the world from the vantage point of Eternity are 'The Dawning' and 'As time one day' but both of them are expressed in much more deliberate Christian and Biblical imagery.

The second interesting characteristic of 'The World' is that Vaughan has used with great skill, generalized morality figures when viewing the world from his eternal vantage-point. 'The doting Lover' (l.8) with his 'silly snares of pleasure' (l.12). 'The darksome States-man hung with weights and woe' (l.16), and 'The fearfull miser' (l.31) are all broad types, instantly recognizable. One becomes so used to personal statement and encounter in Vaughan's poetry that it is a considerable surprise to find him looking at the world as a universal morality, in which he is for most of the poem a fairly detached observer. The only Christian terms he uses are extremely generalized. The 'Treasure' which the Lover has scattered (l.13) is in the most general sense the precious commodity of the Gospels, such as the 'treasure in the heavens that faileth not' (A. V., *Luke*, Ch. 12, v.33).

It is not until the very end of the poem that one recognizes yet again the direct influence of *Revelation*. After his usual contrast between 'dark night' (l.49) and 'true light' (l.50) and a reference to 'grots, and caves' (l.51) which probably owes more to Plato than to Biblical sources, he returns to a picture of Eternity which is very similar indeed to the one he has given us in his other great visionary poems:

The way which from this dead and dark abode
Leads up to God,
A way where you might tread the Sun, and be
More bright than he.
But as I did their madnes so discusse
One whisper'd thus,
This Ring the Bride-groome did for none provide
But for his bride.

(p. 467, ll.53–60)

This passage contains an extremely clever combination of Psalm 19 and the end of the *Book of Revelation*. 'A way where you might tread the Sun' is a most ingenious conceit on parts of verses four, five and six of the psalm, with its famous picture of the sun as 'a bridegroom coming out of his chamber'. But the spirit of the last two lines is surely that of *Revelation*. They give us the entire feeling of that new creation of which John speaks with such supreme confidence in the twenty-first chapter. And they provide a most fitting conclusion to Vaughan's vision in 'The World'. He has been speaking not of any one individual or another. He has taken the greatest care, as we have seen, to generalize mankind and give us a picture of the entire human society. So that his picture of redemption and reconciliation with God in 'the new heaven and a new earth' cannot, by the very terms he has used, be of an individual soul. The only contrast to a corrupt and trivial world he can use is a picture of the whole elect of God, those who by the purity of their lives have been freed from corruption. And he understands perfectly the symbolism of John's vision in *Revelation*. The bride finally represents all the elect of God:

> 'And I John saw the holy city, new Jerusalem, coming down from God out of heaven, prepared as a bride adorned for her husband.'
>
> (A. V. *Revelation*, Ch. 21, v.2)

If the symbol of Eternity is the single most important aspect of Vaughan's work as a religious poet, there should be no mistaking the élite status of that Eternity. 'The World' is certainly no exception to the rest of his work in this respect. None of the corrupt shall enter there, nor any who have neglected to lay up for themselves treasure in Heaven. It is prepared only for those who have absolutely qualified for it, and a great many, including the men of blood of his own generation, are plainly disqualified by the nature of the lives they have led. Only those who have learned how to 'weep and sing' (1.46), which is to suffer, and to celebrate the glory of God, are of the elect. The Judgement of God may never be mentioned directly in 'The World' but it is constantly implied.

By contrast, the elegy 'They are all gone into the world of light!', the third poem in Part Two of his work, stresses not the exclusive nature of Eternity but the boundless freedom of it. It is unquestionably the most celebrated of all his many visions of the world made new, and it is worth asking briefly why this is so. The first reason may well be that it is a much fuller celebration of the sheer joy and perfection of Eternity than any other he has given us; the fact that it may be difficult for human beings to achieve it is never mentioned, or even implied. The second reason may be that he has achieved a fine balance between the particular and the general in his statements. It is firmly rooted in certain particular events and in a specific scene, and yet is able to reach out and apply to any person at any time or place, if the same circumstances of grief apply.

The first stanza shows exactly the same assurance of 'the world of light' as in 'The World', but the mood is much quieter, as befits a meditation on friends he has known:

> They are all gone into the world of light!
> And I alone sit lingring here;
> Their very memory is fair and bright,
> And my sad thoughts doth clear.
>
> It glows and glitters in my cloudy brest
> Like stars upon some gloomy grove,
> Or those faint beams in which this hill is drest,
> After the Sun's remove.
>
> (pp. 483–4, ll.1–8)

'They' is usually thought to refer not only to his favourite brother William but also to other friends killed in the Civil War, or soon afterwards. Very few, if any, of his poems can be separated from the bitterness and tumult of his period, and Vaughan certainly had a wide enough sympathy and also sufficient political inclination to have included in his elegy many who had suffered and died, in what seemed at the time to be a quite hopeless cause.

If it has a particular cause, which it does, it is obviously tied to a particular place; 'this hill' almost certainly localizes it in a place he knew and loved well, either at or very near his home in the Usk Valley. The hill in question would have been either one of the peaks of the Brecon Beacons, or the very familiar Allt yr Ysgair (the Armchair) close by Scethrog where he lived. It is a hill of peculiar beauty and attraction. Just this one phrase strongly personalizes the lament and makes it very much more moving.

But undoubtedly the greatness of the elegy lies in two qualities which have often eluded him. The first is his acceptance of death as a mystery to which he is unwilling to attach any boundaries. He confirms the view of both death and darkness as not only necessary but positive experiences, which we have seen him express in other lyrics in the second part of his work, and especially in 'The Night'. But it is the positive and joyous acceptance of mystery which rings out with such certainty from the verse:

> Dear, beauteous death! the Jewel of the Just,
> Shining nowhere, but in the dark;
> What mysteries do lie beyond thy dust;
> Could man outlook that mark!
>
> (p. 484, ll.16–20)

The second, and even more important quality is his clear expression of the freedom of Eternity. Vaughan has used Biblical parallel, analogy and image far more than most religious poets and this has undoubtedly been the cement of his work. But there are occasions in his lyrics when he becomes too tied to the Biblical symbol to think and feel his own way forward. This elegy is a remarkable example of his ability to construct, albeit on accepted Christian foundations, his own model. The third stanza is an excellent illustration. The environment of those who have reached Eternity is one which liberates them:

> I see them walking in an Air of glory,
> Whose light doth trample on my days:
> My days, which are at best but dull and hoary,
> Meer glimering and decays.
>
> (p. 484, ll.9–12)

The fact of his own 'glimering and decays' is almost totally eclipsed now by the sheer magnificence of his vision. It is exactly the same in his treatment of the bird image (one of his favourites) in the sixth stanza. The fact that we do not know exactly where the bird sings now is unimportant compared with the fact that the bird has flown away in freedom. But there are some intimations of the glory to come:

> And yet, as Angels in some brighter dreams
>   Call to the soul, when man doth sleep:
> So some strange thoughts transcend our wonted theams,
>   And into glory peep.

(p. 484, ll.25–28)

Vaughan's effortless mastery of his material is proved now by his ability to use the intervention of Angels without a single Biblical reference. He has concentrated all his energies upon the complete certainty of his vision of glory.

The closing stanzas of the poem superbly illustrate the confidence of his mood. He prays directly and relevantly for the 'liberty' of God's Eternity. His reference to 'mists' (l.38) may not only mean mental and spiritual blockages. The Usk Valley, splendid though it is, is frequently obscured by mists which blot out the hills in a very few moments. To the very end the poetry remains intimate, and warm in tone, but the prayer he speaks is universal:

> O Father of eternal life, and all
>   Created glories under thee!
> Resume thy spirit from this world of thrall
>   Into true liberty.
>
> Either disperse these mists, which blot and fill
>   My perspective (still) as they pass,
> Or else remove me hence unto that hill,
>   Where I shall need no glass.

(p. 484, ll.33–40)

This very fine lyric is far more than an elegy; it is in the deepest sense a celebration of Eternity, something which, despite all his striving, he rarely achieved in all his poetry. The value of his work here lies surely in the fullness of his revelation; nothing more is needed than that.

'The Palm-tree', five poems later in the collection, is not a poem of the quality of 'They are all gone', but it is a very interesting and poignant illustration of Vaughan's longing for the richness of the new creation, and contains within it a brief but moving vision of Eternity. In selecting the palm-tree as the poem's main symbol, Vaughan is giving, as he has done before in his work, especially in 'The Retreate' a picture of righteousness. But shut out from proper air and light even the palm-tree will die, just as the soul will surely die if it is spoiled by sin and robs itself of the natural grace of God. Two compelling features then emerge.

The first is Vaughan's persistent belief that even the most degraded natures contain within them the instinct for immortality:

> Celestial natures still
> Aspire for home; This *Solomon* of old
> By flowers and carvings and mysterious skill
> Of Wings, and Cherubims, and Palms foretold.
>
> (p. 490, ll.9–12)

If in 'The World' there was a clear statement that only the faithful would be able to enter into God's Eternity, in this poem Vaughan presses the other part of this same truth, that everyone has within them the capacity finally to sue for God's forgiveness. So everyone may win Paradise, though just as certainly not all souls will.

The second intriguing concern is Vaughan's only slightly veiled justification of those who like himself fought against the Puritan cause, and the imposition of the Commonwealth. Once more, one sees how the bitterness of the conflict has erupted into his own life and affected quite deeply his own spirituality. His vision of Eternity is shaped quite unashamedly by his attitude to the bitter war and divisions in his country:

> Here Spirits that have run their race and fought
> And won the fight, and have not fear'd the frowns
> Nor lov'd the smiles of greatness, but have wrought
> Their masters will, meet to receive their Crowns.
>
> (p. 490, ll.16–20)

The implication is clear; they have done 'Their masters will' but not the will of their political masters. But by giving their lives for what they believed was right they have real crowns, not empty political titles. And as if that is not enough, his next stanza underlines the point by hurling back the Puritan title of 'saints' at the Puritans themselves:

> Here is the patience of the Saints: this Tree

Is water'd by their tears, as flowers are fed
With dew by night; but One you cannot see
Sits here and numbers all the tears they shed.

(p. 491, ll.21–24)

It is even possible that Vaughan deliberately leaves open a double meaning on 'One' – Christ, or the late King who was Head of the Church on earth. As in 'The Brittish Church' such an interpretation is certainly possible in the context of the sustained mood of discontent and resentment which is plainly indicated in the latter half of this lyric. Whether there is an intended hint of the late king or not, it is absolutely sure that in 'The Palm-tree' Vaughan's vision of Eternity is born directly out of the conflicts and fears of the Civil War and the scourge of the Royalists which followed it. He quite openly and unashamedly links righteousness with the courage and sacrifice of those who fought in what he believed was the right cause, and paid the price of death, banishment or disgrace. Of such is true sainthood.

In the final poems of his collection Vaughan's thoughts are never far from the idea of Eternity, and now more than ever in his work both the texts and the images of *Revelation* crowd in upon him. There are three poems just before the end of *Silex Scintillans* which amply illustrate this.

The short lyric 'The Throne' is based directly on John's vision of the throne of the Almighty:

'And I saw a great white throne, and him that sat on it, from whose face the earth and the heaven fled away; and there was found no place for them.'

(A. V. *Revelation*, Ch. 20, v.11)

The judgement throne of God compels in Vaughan extreme humility, and the mood is very similar indeed to another short lyric at the end of his work, the exquisite 'Tears'. He expresses simply a humble joy, but there is great confidence here:

When with these eyes clos'd now by thee,
But then restor'd,
The great and white throne I shall see
Of my dread Lord:

(p. 533, ll.1–4)

There is nothing of the anguish of John Donne here. Whatever Vaughan's sadness at the state of the world, whatever the knowledge of his own sin, there is absolutely no doubt that he will finally be 'restor'd'. There are many occasions right through *Silex Scintillans* when he is impatient for eternity, but he never doubts that he will finally see the throne. There is certainly awareness of guilt in his poetry, but in the end, whatever his shortcomings, he feels he is somehow destined for Eternity; that he belongs, in a way Donne very rarely did.

The second interesting feature of 'The Throne' is that he is still aware of the usurpers of religion. His picture of all the earth before the judgement throne of God underscores this:

> And lowly kneeling (for the most
> Stiff then must kneel)
>
> (p. 533, ll.5–6)

This recalls 'Dressing' in its castigation of the Puritans for their blunt refusal to kneel even when they partake of Christ's sacred Body and Blood. The adjective 'stiff' denotes not so much stiffness of body as stiff-necked, having no proper sense of humility.

Finally his conviction that no intellectual prowess will avail at the judgement seat, but only contrition and the capacity to do the will of God is very characteristic of the last poems in his book:

> And should those speechless beggers fail,
> Which oft have won;
> Then taught by thee, I will prevail,
> And say, *Thy will be done!*
>
> (p. 533, ll.13–16)

Two poems later, in 'The Feast' he is yet again contemplating Eternity, but not this time facing the Judgement Throne of God. Here he returns buoyantly to the theme of Holy Communion. But he treats the Sacrament not so much as a means of sustaining man on earth but of giving him a foretaste of heaven. Once more reflecting the mood of the final chapters of *Revelation* the Holy Communion here and now is, as the poem's text makes clear, only a preparation for 'the marriage supper of the Lamb' (A. V. *Revelation*, Ch. 19, v.9):

Come then true bread,
Quickning the dead,
    Whose eater shall not, cannot dye,
Come, antedate
On me that state
    Which brings poor dust the victory.

(p. 534, ll.13–18)

The Communion is also to Vaughan a poignant reminder of the transitoriness of human life and the immense gap between man's experience of God here on earth and the settled joys of Eternity. Using again one of his favourite natural and Biblical images – 'dew' he reveals the extent of his longing for the joys of Heaven:

I victory
Which from thine eye
    Breaks as the day doth from the east,
When the spilt dew,
Like tears doth shew
    The sad world wept to be releast.

(p. 534–5, ll.19–24)

But the anticipation of the joys of a future life which one sensed in 'The Throne' is the key-note of 'The Feast' also, except that the whole mood is one of exaltation. 'Poor dust' may be mentioned twice in the poem, and he still remembers the sadness of the world, but nothing will now stop him celebrating the glories to come. When Vaughan's vision is as certain as this, his verse becomes nothing less than a complete celebration.

O what high joys
The Turtles voice
    And songs I hear! O quickning showers
Of my Lords blood
You make rocks bud
    And crown dry hils with wells & flowers!

(p. 535, ll.49–54)

Vaughan has seized the spirit of the celebratory song of love from the *Song of Solomon* and also taken some of the main images directly from it:

'For, lo, the winter is past, the rain is over and gone;

> The flowers appear on the earth; the time of the singing of birds is come, and the voice of the turtle is heard in our land;
>
> (A. V. Ch. 2, 11–12)

In Vaughan's version the winter of the soul is past, and the blood of Christ waters the land and brings forth Spring. This is nothing less than the world made new. Nature is transformed, and life replaces death, by the act of Holy Communion which prepares directly for the Eternal Feast. But all the nature images are Biblical in origin. 'The Feast' is an excellent example of the way in which Vaughan's vision of Nature restored is obtained quite directly from various Biblical sources.

'The Water-fall', only seven poems from the end of the book, also anticipates the joys of life with God, but is much more concerned with the absolute guarantee of Eternity than either 'The Throne' or 'The Feast'.

Vaughan first of all faces boldly the doubts and fears of those who are frightened by the transitoriness of human life. He does not immediately invoke the Biblical symbolism of water, but presents it, with great beauty, as an image of the soul passing from this world to the next, through the imagined terrors of the grave to the hope of life everlasting: 'The Water-fall' is the catalyst:

> With what deep murmurs through times silent stealth
> Doth thy transparent, cool and watry wealth
> Here flowing fall,
> And chide, and call,
> As if his liquid, loose Retinue staid
> Lingring, and were of this steep place afraid,
> The common pass
> Where, clear as glass,
> All must descend
> Not to an end:
> But quickned by this deep and rocky grave,
> Rise to a longer course more bright and brave.
>
> (p. 537, ll.1–12)

As in many of the visionary poems towards the end of *Silex Scintillans* he gives an open declaration that restoration of the world and the human soul by God requires darkness before there can be light. His images have all the softness and intimacy of 'The Night', but here there is more positive emphasis on light after darkness. Whereas in 'The Night' he ended with the 'deep, but dazling darkness' here he progresses from darkness to light, and his appeal is all the more inviting because it is directed at the 'poor souls' who fear death as the end of all they have known:

> Why, since each drop of thy quick store
> Runs thither, whence it flow'd before,
> Should poor souls fear a shade or night,
> Who came (sure) from a sea of light?
> Or since those drops are all sent back
> So sure to thee, that none doth lack,
> Why should frail flesh doubt any more
> That what God takes, hee'l not restore?
>
> (p. 537, ll.15–22)

Having dealt with the natural doubt of whether anything exists after this mortal experience, Vaughan then rises to a full statement of Eternity which is based directly upon Biblical authority and uses yet again the *Book of Revelation* directly:

> O useful Element and clear!
> My sacred wash and cleanser here,
> My first consigner to those
> Fountains of life, where the Lamb goes?
> What sublime truths, and wholesome themes,
> Lodge in thy mystical, deep streams!
>
> (p. 538, ll.23–28)

The picture of the Lamb is as John has given it in the end of the seventh chapter:

> 'For the Lamb which is in the midst of the throne shall feed them, and shall lead them unto living fountains of waters; and God shall wipe away all tears from their eyes.'

It is the combination of this most vivid picture with the 'Creation' passage which follows it which gives us perhaps the most moving and intense of all Vaughan's visions of eternity, and culminates in the great cry of excitement:

> O my invisible estate,
> My glorious liberty, still late!

Thou art the Channel my soul seeks,
Not this with Cataracts and Creeks.
(p. 538, ll.37–40)

But the claim he makes, intimate and special though it appears to be, comes not from some subjective mystical process. It comes directly from the vision of *Revelation* and the added weight and authority of *Genesis*. 'The Water-fall' like all his finest lyrics is a re-presentation in his own experience of the great prophetic and visionary truths of the Bible.

'The Water-fall' is the last important statement of Eternity which Vaughan has given us in *Silex Scintillans* and it is entirely appropriate that it is the most intimate and personal in its effect. It has no intellectual cleverness, and it is free of the elaborate conceits with occasionally mar his poetry. It expresses with complete conviction a faith in God's power to restore the world and make it new. It is a lyric of great and original beauty.

THE HARMONY OF GOD'S CREATION

The idea of Harmony of all created things, glimpsed here on earth, but brought to a full realization only in Paradise, is the third and final aspect of revelation which runs right through the two books of *Silex Scintillans*. It is implied in a great many poems but in a few it is absolutely central.

One important part of this idea of Harmony of Creation is undoubtedly Vaughan's belief that all living creatures, and even inanimate objects, such as stones, have the positive feeling to respond to the call of their Creator. This particular idea was undoubtedly a central belief in Hermetic philosophy, and there is a good deal of evidence that Vaughan was interested not only in Hermetic Physics and Chemistry (works upon which he translated into English) but also various aspects of the philosophy. It would have been impossible for him not to have known of the main tenets of Hermetic belief because his brother, Thomas, had written so widely on the subject. But the poems which are directly influenced by Hermetic Philosophy are few, and Vaughan is at great pains to fuse any aspects of Hermeticism he selects with the main tenets of Christian belief.

Four poems especially, which are concerned with the theme of the Harmony of God's creation, certainly owe a good deal to Hermetic thought. They are 'Cock-crowing', 'The Starre', 'The Favour' and 'The Bird'. Interestingly, they are all found among the first fifteen poems of *Silex Scintillans* (Part Two), indicating that the influence of Hermetic thought had made a particular mark upon him at that time, probably late 1651 and early 1652.

The first, 'Cock-crowing', is a lyric of great charm in which Vaughan treats the Cock as the precursor of 'Paradise and light' (l.6). In Hermetic astrology the Cock was the bird which responded directly to the Sun, and was believed to attract and draw the rays of the Sun in the first light of morning, so demonstrating a peculiar and magical magnetism. These main ideas are written directly into the first stanza of the poem:

> Father of lights! what Sunnie seed,
> What glance of day hast thou confin'd
> Into this bird? To all the breed
> This busie Ray thou hast assign'd;
> Their magnetisme works all night,
> And dreams of Paradise and light.
>
> (p. 488, ll.1–6)

Vaughan combines two of his most important ideas with great skill in his second stanza. The Cock has the capacity to shake off darkness and usher in the light, and in that instant reveal not only the true glory of the world but become itself an integral part of a unified Creation. It exemplifies the true harmony of all natural objects, and the instinctive response to their Creator's will:

> Their eyes watch for the morning hue,
> Their little grain expelling night
> So shines and sings, as if it knew
> The path unto the house of light.
> It seems their candle, howe'r done,
> Was tinn'd and lighted at the sunne.
>
> (p. 488, ll.7–12)

There is no doubt that the Hermetic philosophers also placed great stress upon the necessity for light. To them it was the origin of all created things, and the essential power of the world was in it. Vaughan's ready use of 'the house of light' exactly fits Hermetic thought. But it would be quite inaccurate to interpret the remainder of the poem as a steady development of Hermetic thought. The dramatic question in the third stanza reveals once again Vaughan's overriding concern with his own place in the scheme of God's Eternity, and it immediately brings us right back to the core of his belief that those who would win Heaven must be entirely vigilant. It is the same message, in essence, as in 'The Dawning', 'The World' and several other of the great visionary poems in which he is obsessed by the vital need to watch for the coming of the Kingdom:

> Shall thy own image think it much
> To watch for thy appearing hour?
>
> (p. 488, ll.15–16)

Through a series of Biblical images – 'immortall light and heat' (l.19), 'frame' (l.20) and 'seed' (l.23) he once again comes to the recognition that only the breaking asunder of the 'Veyle' can make possible the true reconciliation between man and God, without which the harmony of the Universe will never be complete. The bird has the capacity to respond now; but for man it is only possible when he has fully accepted that Christ has shattered for ever the barriers which keep men from God:

> Onely this Veyle which thou has broke,
> And must be broken yet in me,
> This veyle, I say, is all the cloke
> And cloud which shadows thee from me.
>
> (p. 489, ll.37–40)

The same fusion of Hermetic thought and Christian doctrine is seen in 'The Starre', which is placed immediately after it in the collection. The attraction between the earthly body and the star, which is the central statement of the poem is certainly a Hermetic idea, and Vaughan develops the idea to the extent that man may be positively guided by the divine influence of the star:

> Yet, seeing all things that subsist and be,
> Have their Commissions from Divinitie,

And teach us duty, I will see
What man may learn from thee.

(p. 489, ll.9–12)

But the Hermetic idea is carefully subordinated to the principal concept of a God who loves and cares for man. Indeed, the doctrine of personal salvation by a Father who searches and seeks out the soul of man is as strong here as in any poem of Herbert:

This is the Heart he craves; and who so will
But give it him, and grudge not; he shall feel
That God is true, as herbs unseen
Put on their youth and green.

(p. 490, ll.29–33)

He repeats his idea of the correspondence between the herb and the star in 'The Favour' three poems later:

Some kinde herbs here, though low & far,
Watch for, and know their loving star.

(p. 492, ll.7–8)

But the idea of a loving and compassionate God who will 'shine' for him if only he is faithful, eclipses the Hermetic idea. It is highly significant that he ends this tiny but beautiful lyric with a statement of quite traditional seventeenth-century piety:

O let no star compare with thee!
Nor any herb out-duty me!
So shall my nights and mornings be
Thy time to shine, and mine to see.

(p. 492, ll.9–12)

He returns to the idea of the star in the tender and imaginative lyric 'The Bird':

For each inclosed Spirit is a star
Inlighting his own little sphære,
Whose light, though fetcht and borrowed from far,
Both mornings makes, and evenings there.

(p. 496, ll.19–22)

'The Bird' is probably the finest example of his attempt to adapt Hermetic ideas to his Christian ideals and convictions.

There is no doubt that both the 'star' and the 'Birds of light' imagery (l.23) are influenced by Hermeticism but there is no attempt to sustain the ideas for long, or develop them on their own. Instead they become illustrations of general Christian truths, and his images remain consistently Biblical:

> The Turtle then in Palm-trees mourns,
> While Owls and Satyrs howl;
> The pleasant Land to brimstone turns
> And all her streams grow foul.
>
> (p. 497, ll.27–30)

The apocalyptic close of this poem, with its familiar plea for 'the Day-spring' in the final line, echoes both *Psalms* and *Revelation* in its vision of death and destruction which can be expelled only by the light of Christ. Not the light of the star nor of the Bird will save the earth. Only Christ can save man from this apocalypse.

However, the poems which show direct Hermetic influence are extremely interesting in that they reveal clearly Vaughan's search for any clue he can find which can help him understand the Harmony of Creation. But to attribute his belief in such a Harmony mainly to Hermeticism is a misreading of his mind and art. He is perfectly content to let Hermetic concepts enrich his ideas and occasionally colour his imagery. His great delight in darkness in 'The Night' may be increased by his interest in Hermeticism which undoubtedly emphasized the spiritual powers of both darkness and night. But our discussion of 'The Night' has already revealed that the main source of the poem is Biblical and the thought and image of the lyric goes well beyond anything contained in Hermeticism. Exactly the same is true of the Harmony of all Created things. Vaughan's deep conviction that all the elements of the world, animate and inanimate, are capable of showing, in a myriad different ways, the glory of the Creator, is part of a much broader pattern of Christian thought than is found in Hermeticism. His views reflect in great detail some of the main ideas of the New Testament, and especially the writings of Paul.

There are two lyrics in the first part of *Silex Scintillans* which are directly concerned with the Harmony of God's

Creation, and both of them draw a sharp contrast between the restless misery of man and the spontaneous joy and eager anticipation of all other created things.

The first of them, 'And do they so?' is directly Pauline in both thought and image. It is based upon a text from the eighth chapter of *Romans*:

> 'For the earnest expectation of the creature waiteth for the manifestation of the sons of God.'
>
> (A. V., Ch. 8, v.19)

The passage from which this text is taken has long been of interest to Biblical scholars because of its deliberate assertion that 'the creature', by which Paul means the whole world of inanimate entities, is eligible to receive the full liberty of the children of God. Vaughan seizes on this statement with eagerness. Perhaps the single most important phrase in the poem is the first dramatic question with which he opens:

> And do they so? have they a Sense
> Of ought but Influence?
> Can they their heads lift, and expect,
> And grone too? why th'Elect
> Can do no more: my volumes sed
> They were all dull, and dead,
> They judg'd them senslesse, and their state
> Wholly Inanimate.
> Go, go; Seal up thy looks,
> And burn thy books.
>
> (p. 432, ll.1–10)

Predictably some of his images are taken direct from other parts of the eighth chapter. 'Grone' is a clear reference to 'the whole creation groaneth and travaileth in pain together until now.' (v.22) and 'Elect' echoes Paul's question: 'Who shall lay any thing to the charge of God's elect?' (v.33). But the really important truth for Vaughan is that 'the creature' is leading the way to God and is no less important than the very first of the saints whom God has called.

'My volumes' is a general word of contempt for all the conventional wisdom which has asserted that nothing beyond human life is capable of any feeling or response. But it also underlines the uniqueness of this view of the world in traditional Christian literature. This is certainly the most clear and unequivocal statement in the Bible of the value and status of other created things.

The central sections of the poem have all the features of Vaughan's poetry at its most original and imaginative. This is not an exposition but a sheer celebration of the joys of Creation marred only by his perception of his own unworthiness – the model of unregenerate man, as given by Paul in *Romans*:

> I would I were a stone, or tree,
> Or flowre by pedigree,
> Or some poor high-way herb, or Spring
> To flow, or bird to sing!
> Then should I (tyed to one sure state,)
> All day expect my date;
> But I am sadly loose, and stray
> A giddy blast each way;
> O let me not thus range!
> Thou canst not change.
>
> (p. 432, ll.11–20)

The final lines of the poem are a poignant cry that God will not leave him bereft of the promise which all other parts of Nature await with such longing. It is as though Paul's vivid contrasting pictures of the world of the Flesh and the world of the Spirit have exposed the tensions within him; there is probably no lyric of Vaughan's which more movingly conveys the agony of the loss of Eden, which only the blood of Christ can ever redeem:

> O brook it not! thy bloud is mine,
> And my soul should be thine;
> O brook it not! why wilt thou stop
> After whole showres one drop?
> Sure, thou wilt joy to see
> Thy sheep with thee.
>
> (p. 433, ll.35–40)

In the penultimate poem of Part One, there is another striking picture of the restlessness of the human condition, in 'Man'. The theme is very similar to 'And do they so?', and the images of Nature show an inventive novelty which goes far beyond mere cleverness:

> Weighing the stedfastness and state
> Of some mean things which here below reside,
> Where birds like watchful Clocks the noiseless date
> And Intercourse of times divide,
> Where Bees at night get home and hive, and flowrs
> Early, as wel as late,
> Rise with the Sun, and set in the same bowrs;
>
> (p. 477, ll.1–7)

Again Vaughan is heavily influenced by Biblical texts, both from *Psalms* and the Gospels. 'Solomon in all his glory' (A. V., *Matthew*, Ch. 6, v.29) furnishes him with a spectacular proof of the true beauty of the flower, and thus the abiding value of Nature in the working of God's purposes. This lyric is less moving than 'And do they so?', possibly because there is hardly any direct personal reference in it. But it is, for all that, a clear and convincing statement of man the outsider, robbed of the natural joys which the rest of Creation instinctively feels. Indeed, the isolation of man is greater than in the earlier poem. In this world man finds no place in the regularity, order and harmony of creation:

> He knocks at all doors, strays and roams,
> Nay hath not so much wit as some stones have
> Which in the darkest nights point to their homes,
> By some hid sense their Maker gave;
> Man is the shuttle, to whose winding quest
> And passage through these looms
> God order'd motion, but ordain'd no rest.
>
> (p. 477, ll.22–28)

In the second part of *Silex Scintillans* Vaughan's conviction that the whole world of Nature is ready to respond to God's command becomes, if anything, even stronger. And there is a change of emphasis. Nature, in all its manifestations, is increasingly seen as playing a vital role in the intense drama of man's salvation. There is no Nature-worship in Vaughan, and any form of pantheism would be entirely foreign to his view of life and his attitude to God. But there is an increasing emphasis upon the need for man to break his own isolation and become part of the whole of creation, to reject forever his role as an outsider.

To a large extent this desire to belong, to shake off his own deep sense of separateness from the glory of God's creation, seems to have been intensified by the continued desolation of his country under the Puritan regime. Convinced as he was that God's peace and love should enfold the whole of Creation, he longs for that harmony to fill the entire world, including man. This is why in 'Providence', which has already been briefly considered as a prophetic statement, he so conspicuously sets the disordered society of his own age in the context of God's timeless peace and order:

I will not fear what man,
With all his plots and power can;
Bags that wax old may plundered be,
But none can sequester or let
A state that with the Sun doth set
And comes next morning fresh as he.

(p. 505, ll.9–14)

Once again he is thrilled by that most powerful image of 'the creature' waiting expectantly for the coming glory, locked in its own innocence and therefore unaware of all evil machinations of the world:

Poor birds this doctrine sing,
And herbs which on dry hills do spring
Or in the howling wilderness
Do know thy dewy morning-hours,
And watch all night for mists or showers,
Then drink and praise thy bounteousness

(p. 506, ll.31–36)

'The Book' is one of the final poems of *Silex Scintillans*, and an important part of Vaughan's concluding statement at the end of his extraordinarily intense spiritual journey. It is nothing less than a personal testament to the entire Harmony of Creation. Vaughan makes absolutely clear that his theme is the whole relationship between God and the Universe. His opening statement is huge in scope, and formal in style:

Eternal God! maker of all
That have liv'd here, since the mans fall;

The Rock of ages! in whose shade
They live unseen, when here they fade.

(p. 540, ll.1–4)

But 'living' and 'fading' are but two phases of the ultimate reality. Nothing is ever lost or forgotten which had value in Creation; everything is preserved by God's creative love and comprehensive care. With great skill Vaughan interweaves the lives of men and women with the life and purpose of Nature; because both are needed to complete the mystery of God's creation:

Thou knew'st this *papyr*, when it was
Meer *seed*, and after that but *grass*;
Before 'twas *drest* or *spun*, and when
Made *linen*, who did *wear* it then:
What were their lifes, their thoughts & deeds
Whither good *corn*, or fruitless *weeds*.

(p. 540, ll.5–10)

The 'corn' and the 'weeds' clearly echo the Parable of the sower from the thirteenth chapter of Matthew's gospel, and inevitably there is a note of final judgement. Vaughan's vision, as we have noted several times, is rarely without the presence of Judgement. But he certainly does not dwell upon it here. His theme is not the possibility of death but life in all its myriad forms, and as in 'The Water-fall' he deliberately uses symbols of Eternity. The tree, with all its Biblical suggestions of righteousness, is one such symbol:

Thou knew'st this *Tree*, when a green *shade*
Cover'd it, since a *Cover* made,
And where it flourish'd, grew and spread,
As if it never should be dead.

(p. 540, ll.11–14)

Similarly, the beast whose dried skin now furnishes the cover of his book, is a symbol of life:

Thou knew'st this harmless *beast*, when he
Did live and feed by thy decree
On each green thing;

(p. 540, ll.15–17)

This is a clear enough reminder of one of the most lyrical

passages of the *Book of Job* in which the wild ass is pictured as one of the symbols of God's power:

> 'The range of the mountains is his pasture, and he searcheth after every green thing.'
>
> (A. V., *Job*, Ch. 39, v.8)

Vaughan also follows exactly the thought of some of the great books of the Old Testament, especially *Psalms* and *Job* in seeing man as only a tiny speck in God's Universe. Man is still 'meer dust', which implies not only what he was before God formed him, but also corruption and sin. And yet this dust is still important to God and will finally belong to His new Creation:

> Thou knew'st and saw'st them all and though
> Now scatter'd thus, dost know them so.
>
> (p. 540, ll.23–24)

So in this final statement Vaughan links now two of the great strains of *Revelation*, the harmony of creation and the world made new. Only when God finally 'restores' all things, when 'the creature' realizes his expectation, will man also find a place. But the hope is strong now, and he closes with words which plead, in great humility, for his own personal place within that new Creation:

> O knowing, glorious spirit! when
> Thou shalt restore trees, beasts and men,
> When thou shalt make all new again,
> Destroying onely death and pain,
> Give him amongst thy works a place,
> Who in them lov'd and sought thy face!
>
> (p. 540, ll.25–30)

In all Vaughan's greatest lyrics it is the fusion of his extraordinary and intimate Biblical knowledge with his own intensely felt personal experience which constantly surprises and holds us. And 'The Book' is no exception. It is a personal statement which liberates him from the public sorrows of his age, and from the private doubts of his own soul, into a world which can sufficiently take care of both. There is anguish in it, but also peace. Poetically it is one of his best achievements.

* * * * * * *

When one studies the thought and imagery of *Silex Scintillans* in detail it is very easy to see why Vaughan claimed that 'holy writing, must strive (by all means) for *perfection* and true *holyness*, that a *door may be opened to him in heaven*'.[1] To achieve the fullness of revelation becomes for him the basis of his art and the pattern of his life. And the revelation is nothing less than the glory of God.

Certainly no religious poet who has written in English has been more aware of visions of Eternity than Henry Vaughan. But in no sense is he a writer of escapist fantasies, or even a mystic reaching out for 'otherness', rejecting the experience of the world. On the contrary his whole vision of Heaven is illuminated by his experiences on earth, and they are based almost entirely upon his close reading of the most dramatic passages of the Bible. He is fascinated by the apocalyptic writers in particular, and without the *Book of Revelation, Silex Scintillans* would have been a vastly different work.

The *Book of Revelation* gave him not only many of his images and ideas but something of its spirit too. *Revelation* is, after all, a gathering together of so many of the pictures, symbols and prophetic passages of the Bible that it must be regarded as a superb climax of the Scriptures as a whole. Vaughan certainly appears to have seen it as a great climactic song of praise and a blinding vision of Eternity. And if at times the vision is strange and even terrifying Vaughan would have been the last to have forgotten that it was written at a time of great torment and persecution when individual Christians were being hunted and the very existence of the Christian Church was under the gravest threat.

And such, in Vaughan's view, was the state of Britain when he was writing *Silex Scintillans*. The 'captivity', which was explored in the first chapter, is a deep underlying theme throughout, and the hatred, mistrust and downright persecution of those years are in no way incidental to his religious vision. They are an integral part of it. Vaughan pleads for the peace of 'the antient way' at a time when there was no peace. He celebrates the beauty and order of the formal Anglican service at a time when the very Church is despoiled.

[1] Preface to *Silex Scintillans*, p. 392.

He proclaims the integrity and truth of the Anglican religion, with the King as its Head on earth, at a time when the monarch is dead and there is no authority save the Commonwealth and the Puritan Commissioners. He fights a battle for what he sees as genuine spiritual truth and his awareness is constantly sharpened by the political and social pressures of his age.

His vision, then, takes its shape from the very fragments of a broken and divided society. And the spiritual crisis of his own life is matched by the great crisis of his own scattered and beleaguered Church. This is why, in the last poem of *Silex Scintillans* he once more combines the political and the spiritual. Indeed, he could do nothing else. In 'L'Envoy' it is impossible for him ever to forget 'those cancerous, close arts/Which cause solution in all parts' (p. 542, ll.39–40), and his condemnation of 'our haters' (l.29) is as great as ever. And he recognizes that only an extraordinary dispensation of divine grace will ever rescue this situation.

And yet, at the very same time, the most important word in all the last poems is 'Restore'. The great message of *Revelation* for Vaughan is that God will be able to make a new Heaven and new Earth. And despite the remaining bitterness and mistrust revealed in his final poem, he can also give us once more a vision of that restoration:

> Arise, arise!
> And like old cloaths fold up these skies,
> This long worn veyl: then shine and spread
> Thy own bright self over each head,
> And through thy creatures pierce and pass
> Till all becomes thy cloudless glass,
> Transparent as the purest day
> And without blemish or decay,
> Fixt by thy spirit to a state
> For evermore immaculate.
>
> (p. 542, ll.7–16)

We have several times described some of the greatest lyrics of Henry Vaughan as personal testaments. In one sense the whole of his work in *Silex Scintillans* is a testament. It is his courageous attempt to fight his way back to the values and truths which he believes have been driven underground. It is a powerful plea for an end to the shedding of blood, and for a return to the highest justice of man, under God, tempered with His pity, peace and love. And in this testament he lays his own life very much upon the line, setting all his store upon his own spiritual integrity, and trusting, in that period of terrible inner doubt and national tumult, that it will be enough:

> Then keep the antient way!
> Spit out their phlegm
> And fill thy brest with home; think on thy dream;
> A calm, bright day!
> A Land of flowers and spices! the word given,
> *If these be fair, O what is Heaven!*

(p. 488, ll.43–48)